everyday Quinoa

Rena Patten

everyday Quinoa

NEW
HOLLAND

Rena Patten

Contents

This book is dedicated to the Indigenous Andean Community of
South America who have preserved quinoa in its natural state
throughout the ages by passing down their traditional knowledge,
practices and methods. Thank you!

Introduction

There is worldwide recognition now of the importance that quinoa could play in providing a healthy, nutritional and sustainable food source for centuries to come. This life-sustaining seed should be an important part of your diet. Every kitchen should have a packet of quinoa in their pantry. And with this book, you will learn more about the potential of quinoa and how to include it in your everyday diet.

To those of you who already know about quinoa and are now making quinoa part of your everyday meals, I know you are now the converted. But to all that are fairly new or are just starting to learn about this wonderful little grain/seed, welcome to a diet that will be healthy, full of good nutrients and delicious.

When I wrote my first quinoa cook book, *Cooking with Quinoa,* never in my wildest dreams did I think that I would be writing, or should I say cooking, two more quinoa cook books, the second entitled *Quinoa for Families*.

But here we are with book number three filled with all brand-new recipes and with something for everyone. I am once again thrilled to have the opportunity to showcase the many wonderful and beneficial ways to use quinoa—the supergrain—in the kitchen and our everyday diet.

And it is all thanks to the awareness that now exists about this tiny little grain. I will refer to quinoa as a grain throughout this book as this is the term most commonly used but I must point out that quinoa is in fact a seed. I will explain this in more detail later on in the introduction.

The feedback that I am still getting from so many people through my cooking demonstrations or promotional work is more positive than ever. I have been quite overwhelmed at just how many have become aware of and appreciate the huge health benefits of quinoa and have embraced the whole concept of adding it to their daily diet, regardless whether they need to or have to do so.

It is really heartwarming to hear repeatedly from people who have and use *Cooking with Quinoa* and *Quinoa for Families* regularly and how these books have helped them become aware of the many different ways that quinoa in grain, flour and flake form can be prepared in the home kitchen.

People are still telling tell me how much their health and that of their family has improved for the better since including quinoa in their diet. Many have said that they had no previous knowledge of quinoa and their introduction has been through their medical practitioner, dietician or naturopath who suggested they include quinoa in their daily diet.

These comments have been made not only by people who have intolerance to gluten and wheat, but from people of all walks of life who, for one reason or another, need to or just want to change their eating habits for their health.

They have been people who have been diagnosed with or who already have a certain illness where diet seems to play a very important role. Then there are other people that have been looking for a general alternative to eating rice and pasta and have actually lost weight by switching to quinoa. They also claim to be able to better manage and control their weight by continuing to use quinoa. And then, of course then there are people that eat quinoa simply because they like it.

I am also very surprised at the number of people who have an intolerance to rice and have therefore welcomed the opportunity to not only have a substitute to use but a substitute that has numerous beneficial health qualities and that is actually good for you.

When I first decided to write a cookbook about quinoa, my main purpose was to bring awareness of the existence of this grain and particularly the health benefits associated with it and show the different ways that it can be used in your cooking. A lot of people I spoke to were not even aware that you could get quinoa in flour and flake form: they only knew about the grain and even then only because they had been told about it by their health care professional.

I was so surprised to hear from so many that they were sprinkling the grain, without cooking it, on their breakfast cereal as they had no idea how to prepare it.

I was not surprised, however, to hear that they did not find this method very palatable and according to many, my quinoa cook books have now changed all of that.

It is really a very useful ingredient to use, particularly when cooking at the same time for a group of people with varied dietary needs.

As with my two previous quinoa books I have only used quinoa in grain, flake or flour form as a main ingredient in all the recipes. At no time have I used any other grain or form of gluten, wheat or rice. I want to show you that you can create delicious tasting and more nutritional meals using quinoa in the three different forms and that you don't have to add products containing gluten/wheat for them to work or taste good.

As with all recipes in general, feel free to interchange ingredients such as herbs and spices to suit your taste or their availability in your kitchen at the time of cooking. Recipes should be used as guides and don't have to be precisely followed to the letter except for baking where you need to be a little more precise. I have used common everyday ingredients that are readily available at your local supermarket or greengrocer. They are not hard to find nor do you have to embark on a major travel expedition to find them. I have also included a few recipes from my previous book, *Quinoa for Families*. The recipes I chose are ones I think really are everyday recipes using quinoa and I wanted to add them as a bonus to this book.

I tend to use canned legumes and pulses a lot as I find them so easy and convenient. I always have some on hand in my pantry as well as frozen spinach and peas in my freezer.

What is quinoa?
(pronounced keen-wah)

You may be asking what exactly is quinoa? quinoa, pronounced 'keen-wah', is a tiny little grain, but not just any grain. It is a grain that is considered to be almost a complete food, being very high in protein, full of vitamins, totally gluten-, wheat- and cholesterol-free, usually organic and of absolutely great benefit to everyone's diet. It is very easy to prepare and tastes absolutely delicious.

In a nutshell, quinoa is a complete source of protein and has all the essential amino acids, trace elements and vitamins you need to survive.

It is an ancient seed native to the Andes Mountains in South America. It has been around for over 5,000 years and is known to have been a staple food of the ancient civilisation of the Incas having sustained them for centuries.

It was used to supplement their diet of potatoes and corn. It was commonly referred to as the 'mother grain' or 'gold of the Incas' and was considered sacred. It is still considered a very important food in the South American kitchens. I have always referred to quinoa as the Supergrain of the Century.

As stated earlier, although most commonly referred to as a grain, quinoa is in actual fact a seed. It is the seed of a leafy plant called *Chenopodium quinoa* of the Chenopodium/Goosefoot plant family and is distantly related to the spinach plant. I like to refer to it as a grain because to me it gives people a rough idea about the size of this grain, whereas the term 'seed' could imply that it is similar in size to the seed in citrus fruit or an olive or an avocado for instance.

Quinoa is a pure and complete grain and almost the perfect food as the degree of nutrition in each tiny grain is regarded as being quite potent. It has the highest amount of protein of any grain and this unusually high amount of protein is actually a complete protein containing all nine essential amino acids, the only grain to contain all nine essential amino acids. The quality of this protein has been likened, by the World Health Authority, as being the closest to milk.

The amino acid composition is extremely well balanced and has a particularly high content of the amino acid lysine which is essential in our diet for tissue repair and growth. Quinoa is a must for vegans and vegetarians who may be concerned about the level of protein in their daily diet.

It is also a very good source of manganese, magnesium, potassium, phosphorous, copper, zinc, vitamin E, vitamin B6, riboflavin, niacin and thiamine. It has more calcium than cow's milk, is an excellent antioxidant, is rich in dietary fibre and has more iron than any other grain. It also has the highest content of unsaturated fats and a lower ratio of carbohydrates than any other grain plus a low glycemic index (GI) level. The health benefits to be gained from using this grain are truly enormous.

Quinoa has a huge range of uses and lends itself beautifully to so many dishes. When cooked it has a very delicate texture and is lovely in soups, sweets, makes wonderful salads, pasta, breads, and delicious vegetarian and non-vegetarian meals. You can also make pastry for pies using quinoa flour—bear in mind though that pastry made with quinoa flour may go a little soggy quicker than if you were using normal gluten flour.

I consider quinoa to be a perfect food for coeliac sufferers, vegans and vegetarians.

My philosophy in food has always been that people with special dietary requirements should not miss out and should be able to enjoy most of the food that people without special dietary requirements enjoy. Now with quinoa and knowledge of the many different ways that it can be prepared, people can do just that!

I think of and use quinoa as a special natural food, nature's very own superfood. It is very easy to prepare, easy to digest and most enjoyable to eat. It is very light on the stomach and you don't tend to feel at all heavy after eating a meal made with quinoa. I also find certain sweets prepared with the quinoa flour can be lighter than those prepared with normal wheat flour.

To those who are gluten- and wheat-intolerant, quinoa is a food that can offer you a greater variety of ideas for your everyday table and for those special meals that you can offer your guests.

What does quinoa look like?

The grain itself is tiny and round with a fine band around it ending in what looks like a minute 'tail'. As it cooks the 'tail' spirals out and almost detaches itself. It becomes very distinct from the rest of the grain in the shape of an outer white ring that is clearly visible. When cooked the grain becomes very soft in the centre while the 'tail' retains a bit of crunch giving it a texture all of its own.

When the grain is cooked it has a very delicate texture and it expands to almost four times its original volume.

There are many different varieties of quinoa and it is available in grain form, flakes and flour, making it suitable for cooking in many different ways. The colour of the grain can vary from white (opaque) or pale yellow to red, purple, brown and black. The recipes in this book extensively use the grain, flake or flour form of this wonderful grain in one way or another so as to show you just how easy it is to use this supergrain in so many different ways.

It is available at most health food stores and in the health food section of the larger supermarkets. Some shops also stock quinoa milk; it is however quite expensive and not that readily available. Toasted quinoa is also available but why not make your own (see recipe)? You can keep a jar of it in your pantry to sprinkle on your porridge, ice cream or use instead of croutons in your soups or sprinkled over your salads for added crunch. Homemade toasted quinoa tends to keep for quite a while stored in a glass jar with a tight-fitting lid. You can also buy puffed quinoa.

quinoa flour

quinoa flakes

Cooked quinoa is very distinctive in both taste and appearance and stands out from other grains. It has a lovely, slightly nutty taste that is unique and can be substituted for just about any other grain. It can be used as an accompaniment to a meal as you would use rice for example or you can use it with other ingredients to make up a complete meal.

The distinct nutty taste is more pronounced in the flour, giving it quite an earthy aroma. The flour can also be slightly bitter, which I find can be counterbalanced by the other sweeter or aromatic ingredients used in a recipe. The flakes are great used as a substitute for normal breadcrumbs, especially for stuffings and coatings. The slightly bitter taste that you find in the flour and the flakes is attributed to the fact that we are not able to rinse them before using as we do the grain. You will also find that any of the recipes that use the flour in large quantities, such as a cake, will always be slightly darker than if you were to use normal gluten flour.

How to prepare quinoa

Quinoa grows in arid climates, at high altitudes and very poor soil. It is suggested that the survival of this plant over the centuries could be attributed to a soapy-like substance called 'saponin', which creates a bitter coating on the grain and protects it from the harsh, high-altitude weather as well as any birds or insects.

This bitter soapy coating must be removed before cooking. Although most grain comes pre-washed and ready to cook. It is still a good idea to rinse it thoroughly before use to remove any residue of 'saponin'. I always tell people that they must rinse the grain before cooking.

Simply place the quinoa into a fine sieve and rinse under cold running water. After thoroughly wetting the quinoa, rub it lightly between your fingertips, drain well and it is ready to cook. Make sure that you do use a very fine sieve as the grains are so tiny and will otherwise go straight through a standard colander or strainer.

Quinoa cooks very quickly simmered in water, stock, juice or milk. One part quinoa, two parts liquid and 10 minutes in the saucepan are usually all that is needed to prepare quinoa as a basic cooked grain. However, you may need to cook the quinoa a little longer if the liquid is denser than water, such as a sauce, stock or milk. And also the darker grains, the red and black varieties, take a little longer to cook and tend to retain a little bit more of a crunch. The length of the cooking time can also vary depending on the brand and age of the grain. Resting the cooked quinoa covered, for 10–15 minutes after cooking, will ensure it is softer and fluffier. Use a fork to fluff up the quinoa after it has been cooked.

Quinoa can be cooked in the microwave, although this is not my preferred method—I find it a bit too fiddly and it seems to take longer. To cook quinoa in the microwave place 1 part quinoa to 2 parts liquid in a microwave-proof dish and cook on high for 7 minutes; stir, then cover with plastic wrap and stand for 7–8 minutes. Depending on your microwave you may need to vary the cooking time. You can also cook quinoa in a rice cooker in the same way that you would on the stove top. One part quinoa to two parts water cooked on the rice setting then rest, covered, for 5–10 minutes.

For an added nutty taste, you can toast the quinoa before cooking. Rinse and drain the quinoa well, then dry roast in a small non-stick frying pan. When the grains start to pop, remove the pan from heat and transfer the quinoa to a saucepan with 2 parts liquid, bring to the boil, then reduce the heat and simmer, covered, for 10 minutes.

You can also sprout quinoa by placing 1 part rinsed quinoa with 3 parts water in a jar with a lid and soak for about 2 hours; drain and rinse, then return to the jar with the lid on and leave to sprout. You must rinse them at least twice per day. They are very tiny sprouts and should be ready in about 2–3 days but must be eaten immediately as they do not last. You can use the sprouts in salads.

To prepare the salads from this book you will need to cook the quinoa first, cool completely and then combine with the other ingredients.

I make a lot salads using quinoa so I tend to cook a large batch of the grain and leave it in the refrigerator to use as I need it. Quinoa cooked in water will keep in the refrigerator for up to a week. For most of the other recipes in this book where the grain is used, the grain is actually cooked with the other ingredients, making them one-pot meals. Which coloured grain you wish to use in your cooking is totally up to you. I have specified a colour in only a few recipes and that was done purely for visual appeal.

Cooking appliances

It is important to remember that all cooking appliances, especially ovens, vary in their cooking time so you may need to experiment with your own to work out the correct cooking time.

Also cooking time can vary depending on the grain used, temperature of your cooking appliance and, believe it or not, even the type and size of saucepan used.

For the one-pot meals I find the best utensil to use is a large deep wide-surfaced frying pan with a lid. It not only holds a large quantity of ingredients but it also distributes and cooks the quinoa with all the other ingredients more evenly over a larger cooking surface.

Breakfast

Note *These bars are great for breakfast on the run or for a quick but satisfying and nourishing snack. Pack them into school and work lunch boxes, take them to picnics or have them as an after-sport snack.*

Breakfast Bars

Makes 16

¾ cup quinoa flour

1 teaspoon gluten-free baking
  powder

1 cup quinoa flakes

1 teaspoon ground cinnamon

¾ cup brown sugar

4 oz/125 g dried cranberries

4 oz/125 g cup dried apricots,
  chopped

3 oz/90 g golden raisins

4 oz/125 g sunflower seeds

2 oz/60 g slivered almonds,
  chopped

2 oz/60 g butter

⅓ cup honey

1 teaspoon vanilla bean paste

2 extra large eggs, lightly beaten

Preheat the oven to 350°F/180°C and lightly grease a 12 x 7 ½ in/29 x19 cm slice tin then line with baking paper. Greasing the tin first helps the paper stay in place.

Sift flour and baking powder into a large bowl then stir in the quinoa flakes, cinnamon and sugar. Mix well, making sure you break up any lumps in the sugar.

Add the cranberries, apricots, raisins, sunflower seeds and almonds. And mix well to combine.

Place butter and honey into a small saucepan and stir over low heat until butter has melted, and then stir in the vanilla.

Pour the melted butter and the eggs over the flour and fruit mixture and mix really well pressing the mixture together so it is well combined and not dry.

Using the back of a spoon, press mixture firmly into the prepared tin then bake for about 20–25 minutes until golden.

Remove from the oven and leave to cool in the tin for about 15 minutes and then cut into desired sized bars. Leave to cool in the tin for a little longer then carefully remove the slice with the paper and place on a cooling rack to cool completely.

Note *This is one of those mixes that is good to have on hand as it is not only great for breakfast. You can grab a handful of this at anytime. Good in school or work lunches. If you don't have maple syrup you can use golden syrup instead. Keep an eye on it while it is in the oven as it can burn easily. I have used the red quinoa in this recipe purely for the added crunch that you get from the darker grain.*

Crunchy Breakfast Mix

Makes 8 cups

Place quinoa into a small saucepan with the water. Bring to the boil, reduce the heat and simmer for 10 minutes until all the water is absorbed. Remove from the heat, uncover and cool completely.

Preheat oven to 325°F/160°C and line two large baking trays with non-stick baking parchment/paper.

In a large bowl, mix together the quinoa flakes, cooled quinoa grain, almonds, pepitas, sunflower and sesame seeds, cinnamon and nutmeg.

Add the vanilla, maple syrup, brown sugar, honey and oil and mix really well, as you want all the ingredients to be completely coated.

Spread the mixture out evenly over the two trays in a single layer and bake for about 30–40 minutes until crisp and crunchy and a rich golden colour. Stir once or twice through the baking time making sure you keep the mix evenly distributed in the tray.

Remove from the oven and cool, then stir in the raisins and cranberries and store in an airtight container when completely cold. Serve with milk or yoghurt or sprinkle over porridge.

¾ cup red quinoa, rinsed and drained

1½ cups water

1½ cups quinoa flakes

4 oz/125 g whole blanched almonds

2½ oz/75 g pepitas/pumpkin seeds

2½ oz/75 g sunflower seeds

2 oz/60 g sesame seeds

2 teaspoons ground cinnamon

½ teaspoon ground nutmeg

1 tablespoon vanilla

⅓ cup maple syrup

⅓ cup light brown sugar, tightly packed

⅓ cup honey

2 tablespoons vegetable or extra light olive oil

5 oz/150 g golden raisins

4 oz/125 g dried cranberries

Note This is the perfect leisurely Sunday breakfast, especially if you are having guests. It's also great served for brunch, lunch or a light supper. You can replace the bacon with ham or chorizo sausage or leave the meat out altogether for a lovely vegetarian option.

Asparagus and Bacon Frittata

Serves 6

¾ cup quinoa, rinsed and drained

1½ cups water

1 oz/30 g butter

6 scallions/spring onions, sliced

4 rashers bacon, rind removed and
    cut into strips

2 bunches asparagus, trimmed and
    sliced

10 extra large eggs

½ cup milk

Salt and freshly ground black
    pepper

2 tablespoons chives, chopped

Place quinoa into a small saucepan with the water. Bring to the boil, reduce the heat, cover and simmer for 10 minutes until all the water is absorbed.

While quinoa is cooking, melt the butter in a medium-sized frying pan and cook scallions and bacon until the scallions are soft and bacon is golden and starting to crisp up.

Add the asparagus and cook for 2–3 minutes until tender but still a little crunchy.

In the meantime, whisk the eggs with the milk and season with salt and pepper to taste.

When the asparagus are ready, stir in the quinoa then pour the egg mixture over the top and gently mix to combine.

Cook on low-medium heat until the frittata is set underneath but still runny on the top.

Sprinkle the chives over the top of the frittata then place the frying pan under a hot preheated grill and cook until the frittata is set and golden.

Allow the frittata to rest for 2–3 minutes before loosening with a spatula and slowly sliding onto a serving dish, or leave in the pan if you prefer (less washing up!).

Note *You can make this with full or reduced fat milk or replace with any lactose-free milk.*

Creamy Apple and Cinnamon Porridge

Serves 4–6

Coarsely grate the apples, keeping the skin on, and place into a medium-sized saucepan with the water and sugar.

Bring to the boil then reduce the heat and simmer for 5 minutes to soften the apples.

Add the quinoa flakes, milk, vanilla and cinnamon to the saucepan and stir well. Start off with the lower amount of cinnamon and sugar, and increase according to taste.

Bring to the boil on medium heat. Once boiling, reduce the heat to low and simmer for about 5–7 minutes until the porridge is thick and creamy.

Serve with extra milk if needed and a good sprinkle of toasted quinoa (see recipe).

2 apples

1 cup water

2–3 tablespoons brown sugar

1 cup quinoa flakes

3 cups milk

1 teaspoon vanilla extract

½–1 teaspoon ground cinnamon

Note *For a vegetarian option, you can omit the ham and replace with finely chopped spinach or cooked corn kernels.*

Savoury Buttermilk Pancakes

Serves 4

1½ cups quinoa flour

1 teaspoon baking powder

1 teaspoon baking soda/bicarbonate
    of soda

Salt and freshly cracked black
    pepper

3 extra large eggs

1 tablespoon English mustard

1¾ cups buttermilk

7 oz/200 g ham, chopped

9 oz/250 g ricotta cheese

3 tablespoons parmesan cheese,
    grated

2 tablespoons chopped fresh
    chives

Butter, for cooking

Maple syrup (optional)

Sift together the quinoa flour, baking powder and baking soda then stir in the salt and pepper.

Whisk together the eggs and mustard, then mix in the milk.

Using a whisk, mix together the dry ingredients with the wet ingredients until you have a lump-free smooth batter, then stir in the ham, ricotta and parmesan cheeses and the chives. If possible, leave the batter to rest for at least 10 minutes.

Heat a little butter in a non-stick pan on medium heat until it starts to bubble, pour about ⅓ cup of the pancake mixture into the pan and lightly spread to form a circle.

Cook until bubbles form on the top of the pancake then gently flip over and cook on the other side for about 30 seconds.

Remove from pan and repeat with the remaining batter.

Serve pancakes hot with a drizzle of maple syrup.

Note *These muffins are great for school lunches. This recipe makes a lot of mini muffins but they freeze really well. Just pop a frozen one in their school lunches. They are lovely eaten warm or cold and will remain fresh and moist for three to four days—kids love them.*

Mini Banana Muffins

Makes 48 mini muffins

Preheat oven to 335°F/170°C and line two 24-cup mini muffin tin with paper cases.

Mash the bananas with the lemon juice and set aside.

Sift together the flour, sugar, baking soda, baking powder and salt into a large bowl. Pour milk into a jug then lightly beat in the eggs, vanilla and oil.

Make a well in the centre of the dry ingredients and slowly pour in the liquid ingredients, mixing as you go until all the ingredients are combined.

Gently fold in the bananas; do not over mix.

Spoon the mixture into the prepared muffin tin, filling each case fairly close to the top and cover with a thin slice of banana, if using.

Bake for about 20 minutes until they have risen, are golden and firm to the touch, and skewer comes out clean when tested.

2 overripe bananas

2 teaspoons lemon juice

2 cups quinoa flour

1 cup superfine/caster sugar

1 level teaspoon baking soda/ bicarbonate of soda

½ level teaspoon gluten-free baking powder

½ teaspoon salt

¾ cup milk

2 large eggs

2 teaspoons vanilla paste or extract

¼ cup vegetable or extra light olive oil

1 banana, for garnish (optional)

Note You can use whatever other berries you prefer. Alternatively if you don't want to make a sauce you can stir 9oz/250 g of your favourite berry into the batter before cooking and serve with a drizzle of maple syrup.

Ricotta Pancakes with a Berry Sauce

Serves 4

1½ cups quinoa flour

1 teaspoon baking powder

1 teaspoon baking soda/bicarbonate
    of soda

2 tablespoons sugar

3 extra large eggs

1½ teaspoon vanilla bean paste or
    extract

1¾ cups buttermilk

14 oz/400 g ricotta cheese

Butter, for cooking

Maple syrup (optional)

BERRY SAUCE

17½ oz/500 g frozen blueberries or
    berries of your choice

¼ cup granulated sugar

Sift together the quinoa flour, baking powder and baking soda, then stir in the sugar.

Whisk together the eggs and vanilla, then mix in the buttermilk.

Using a whisk, mix together the dry ingredients with the wet ingredients until you have a lump-free, smooth batter, then stir in the ricotta cheese.

Heat a little butter in a non-stick pan on medium heat until it starts to bubble, pour in about ⅓ cup of the pancake mixture into the pan and lightly spread into a circle.

Cook until bubbles form on the top of the pancake then gently flip over and cook on the other side for about 30 seconds.

Remove from pan and repeat with the remaining batter.

Serve pancakes stacked on top of one another with the berry sauce or alternatively you can serve them with a drizzle of maple syrup and, if you like, some natural yoghurt.

To make the Berry Sauce: place frozen berries in a medium saucepan with the sugar and stir over a low heat. Once the berries have defrosted and sugar has melted and the mixture starts to bubble, gently simmer for about 2–3 minutes. Avoid stirring the berries with a spoon: just lightly toss the pan every now and then.

You may need to vary the amount of sugar used depending on the tartness of the berries and your personal taste.

Fruit Smoothies

Serves 1-2

Place all the ingredients into a blender and blend until thick and smooth.
For added protein, add an egg white. You can use apple juice instead of the
milk or a bit of both. You can replace the frozen berries for other fruit such as
bananas, mango and peaches or any fruit that can be placed in the freezer to
have on hand and throw into a smoothie.

1 cup frozen berries

⅓ cup quinoa flakes

1–2 tablespoons honey

1 cup low-fat milk

¼ cup water

1 teaspoon vanilla extract

The Super Green Drink

Serves 1-2

Place all ingredients into a blender and blend until thick and smooth. If too
thick, add a little water. As with the fruit smoothie recipe above, you can
vary the green leaves used according to your taste. For example, you can use
spinach and cucumber instead of the kale. The yoghurt tends to add a little
creamy richness to the drink; however, it tastes just as good without it if you
would prefer to leave it out.

*2 handfuls fresh kale, washed and
  chopped*

*1 large green apple, left unpeeled,
  remove the core and seeds*

½ cup quinoa flakes

*2 tablespoons honey or agave
  syrup*

2 cups apple juice

2 celery stalks, roughly chopped

Small handful of fresh basil

Juice ½–1 lemon

*2 tablespoons natural Greek
  yoghurt (optional)*

Ice cubes

Note *These are delicious eaten warm or cold so are ideal for a breakfast on the run. You can substitute bacon for the chorizo or, for a vegetarian option, omit the meat altogether. I tend to make the vegetarian option a lot as my daughters are vegetarians, but these are equally enjoyed by all the non-vegetarians we serve them to.*

Zucchini, Chorizo and Cheese Muffins

Makes 12 muffins

1 cup quinoa flour

1 teaspoon gluten-free baking powder

1 teaspoon baking soda/bicarbonate of soda

2 chorizo sausages, chopped into small pieces

12 oz/350 g zucchini/courgettes, coarsely grated

1 onion, coarsely grated

1 cup grated tasty/matured cheese

5 eggs, lightly beaten

⅓ cup light olive oil

Salt and freshly ground pepper

Preheat oven to 350°F/180°C and lightly grease a 12-hole muffin tin.

Sift the flour, baking powder and baking soda together and set aside.

Lightly brown the chopped chorizo in a non-stick frying pan, drain and discard any fat that may be left in the pan then place into a bowl with the zucchini, onion and cheese.

Mix in the eggs and oil then fold in the flour mixture and season with salt and pepper.

Pour the mixture into the prepared muffins tins and bake for about 20–25 minutes until golden and cooked when tested with a skewer.

These can be prepared the night before and re-heated for breakfast.

Note *This is really great to have in your pantry to use on or over just about anything you like. You can sprinkle it over your porridge, ice cream, stewed fruit, fruit salad, over soups in place of bread croutons or as a crunchy topping over salads.*

Toasted Quinoa

Makes about 2 cups

1 cup quinoa, rinsed and drained

2 cups water

Place quinoa into a small saucepan with the water. Bring to the boil, reduce the heat, cover and simmer for 10 minutes until all the water is absorbed. Take off the heat and leave covered for 10 minutes.

Remove from the pan and spread out onto a baking tray and leave to cool completely. This is to remove as much moisture as possible.

When the quinoa has cooled, heat a large non-stick frying pan until fairly hot on medium-high heat. You will need a frying pan that has a large surface cooking area.

Spread the quinoa in the pan and dry-roast until you get a lovely crunchy and golden quinoa. This will take about 15–20 minutes and you will need to toss the quinoa in the pan regularly.

You will notice it starting to take on some colour after about 8–10 minutes and it is at that point that you want to keep an eye on it as once it starts to toast the process doesn't take very long.

Alternatively, you can toast the quinoa in the oven. Preheat the oven to 400°F/200°C and once the quinoa has cooled after boiling, spread on to a baking tray that has been lined with non-stick baking parchment/paper and bake, stirring regularly, for about 10–15 minutes until you reach the level of toastiness that you like.

I prefer the stove-top method as I have more control over the cooking process; however, the end result is the same.

Remove the toasted quinoa from the frying pan or the oven and allow to cool completely then store in a glass jar with a tight lid.

It will keep in the jar for some time.

Soups

Note This one of those 'feel good' soups. It feels very cleansing and you feel good when eating it and actually feel it is doing you good. This one of my favourite soups and so quick to make. You can either make this soup simply as is or if you prefer you can add some finely sliced fresh raw chicken to the stock at the start. I always make a double quantity.

Asian-style Soup

Serves 4

8 cups chicken or vegetable stock

1 stalk lemongrass, bruised

2 star anise

1 tablespoon grated fresh ginger

1 large clove garlic, peeled and
   lightly smashed

⅔ cup quinoa grain, rinsed and
   drained

3 oz/90 g fresh shiitake mushrooms,
   sliced

1 small bunch choy sum or bok
   choy (pak choy), washed well
   and cut into strips, chopped
   (about 4 cups)

4 scallions/spring onions, sliced

1 red chilli, sliced

2 tablespoons fish sauce

2–3 tablespoons tamari soy sauce

1 cup water or stock, extra

Fresh bean sprouts, for garnish

Fresh cilantro/coriander leaves, for
   garnish

Lime juice, to taste

Bring the stock to the boil in a large saucepan with the lemongrass, star anise, ginger and garlic.

Add the quinoa, reduce the heat, cover and simmer on low heat for about 15 minutes until the quinoa is almost cooked.

Add the mushrooms, choi sum, scallions, chilli, fish sauce and soy sauce, bring back to the boil, reduce the heat and simmer for another 5 minutes. Add an extra cup of stock or water if you feel at this stage that the soup may be too thick.

Remove the lemongrass and serve garnished with bean sprouts, fresh cilantro leaves and lime juice.

Note *Thigh cutlets are the thigh with the back rib part of the bone removed and only the larger thigh bone left in. Because there is only one bone, I find using stock instead of water will give a far richer and tastier soup. I do like to use chicken thigh cutlets in this recipe as I feel thighs are better for soups and with just the larger bone in them the risk of finding smaller bones in the soup is less. But of course you can use whatever chicken pieces you prefer.*

Creamy Chicken and Leek Soup

Serves 6

In a large saucepan, melt the butter and heat the oil until hot, then sauté the leeks, celery and onion until they soften and collapse and just start to take on some colour.

Remove the skin from the chicken (optional) and add to the pot with the stock, cloves and peppercorns.

Bring to the boil, reduce the heat and simmer for about 30–40 minutes until chicken is cooked. Skim and remove any froth that rises during cooking.

Remove the chicken from the pot and set aside. Puree the soup and bring back to the boil.

When the soup is boiling, add the quinoa and season with salt. Reduce the heat, cover and simmer for about 20–30 minutes until the quinoa is cooked.

In the meantime, if you have left the skin on during cooking, remove the skin from the chicken and shred the meat into pieces.

Add the shredded chicken and cream to the soup and stir well. Taste and adjust the seasoning if necessary then continue to simmer on very, very low heat for 5 minutes until the chicken and cream have heated through.

Serve with a good grind of freshly cracked black pepper.

1 tablespoon butter

1–2 tablespoons extra virgin olive oil

2 large leeks, washed and sliced

3 celery stalks, roughly chopped

1 brown onion, chopped

6 chicken thigh cutlets about 2 lb 13 oz/1.25 kg

8 cups chicken stock or water

Pinch of ground cloves

10–12 peppercorns

¾ cup red quinoa, rinsed and drained

Salt and pepper

½ cup cream

Note This is another one of my favourite soups. I usually use a stick blender to puree my soups: I find this method a lot easier and it certainly cuts down on the washing up.

Roasted Red Pepper and Basil Soup

Serves 6–8

3 lb 5 oz/1.5 kg red bell peppers/
    capsicums

2 large red onions, peeled

1 head garlic, cut in half

Extra virgin olive oil

Salt and freshly cracked black
    pepper

8 cups hot vegetable or chicken
    stock

Zest of 1 lemon

¾ cup quinoa grain, rinsed and
    drained

3–4 tablespoons finely chopped
    basil

Natural Greek yoghurt, for
    serving

Preheat oven to 400°F/200°C. Line a large baking tray with non-stick baking parchment/paper.

Cut peppers in half, remove the seeds and the membrane, then cut into large chunks.

Peel and thickly slice the onions and place onto the baking tray with the peppers and the cut and unpeeled garlic.

Drizzle the vegetables with some olive oil and season well with salt and pepper.

Using your hands, mix until all the vegetables are well coated with the oil and the seasonings.

Place in the oven to roast for about 40–50 minutes until the peppers are tender and slightly charred. If you prefer, you can at this stage remove the skins from the peppers: they will come off very easily. I always leave them on as I find they are not noticeable and puree really well plus they add some extra texture to the soup. Once cooked, remove the skin from the garlic, then puree the vegetables and garlic with the stock using a food processor or stick blender.

Pour puree into a saucepan and bring to the boil. When soup starts boiling add the lemon zest and quinoa, reduce the heat, cover and cook on low heat for about 20 minutes until the quinoa is tender and cooked.

Stir in the basil and leave to stand for about 10–15 minutes.

Serve with a good squeeze of lemon juice and a dollop of yoghurt.

Note *I have used canned tomatoes in this recipe only for ease of preparation as most people usually have these in their pantry and also for the times when fresh tomatoes are too expensive. By all means use fresh if you can. Substitute the tinned variety with 3 lb 5 oz/1½ kg of fresh tomatoes that have been quartered. Remember to pick out the skins from the saucepan once tomatoes are cooked before you puree the soup*

Tomato, Leek and Cilantro Soup

Serves 4–6

Dry-roast the coriander and cumin seeds in a small non-stick frying pan for about a minute until fragrant. Remove from heat immediately so they do not burn and pound into a powder in a mortar and pestle, set aside.

Heat oil in a large saucepan and cook onion and leek until soft. Add the garlic and ground coriander and cumin and cook for about 1 minute.

Add the tomatoes, sugar, stock, fresh cilantro, salt and pepper, bring back to the boil, reduce heat and simmer for about 30 minutes.

Puree soup, return to the saucepan and add the quinoa and hot water. Bring back to the boil, reduce heat, cover and simmer for 15 minutes.

Garnish with the fresh chives and serve with a squeeze of lime juice.

1 tablespoon dried coriander seeds

1 teaspoon cumin seeds

2 tablespoons olive oil

1 large onion, chopped

1 leek, washed and sliced

4 cloves garlic, chopped

4x 15 oz/440 g cans diced Italian tomatoes, undrained

1–2 teaspoons sugar, depending on acidity of tinned tomatoes

6 cups hot vegetable stock

1 large handful fresh cilantro/ coriander, roughly chopped including the stalks and roots

Salt and pepper

⅔ cup quinoa grain, rinsed and drained

½ cup boiling water

Chives, chopped, for garnish

Lemon or lime juice

Note *This is a thick and hearty soup, wonderful for those cold wintery days. If you think the soup may be too thick add a little hot water.*

Zucchini and Bacon Soup

Serves 4–6

2 tablespoons extra virgin olive oil

10½ oz/300 g bacon, rind removed and cut into pieces

2 large onions, finely chopped

2 tablespoons tomato concentrate/ paste

2 lb 4 oz/1 kg zucchini/courgette, coarsely grated

2 cloves garlic, finely chopped

8 cups hot beef stock

Salt and freshly ground pepper

¾ cup quinoa, rinsed and drained

2–3 tablespoons balsamic vinegar

Buffalo mozzarella, to serve

Heat oil in a large saucepan and sauté bacon on medium heat until it is lightly browned.

Add the onion and cook until soft. Stir in the tomato concentrate and cook for about 2 minutes.

Stir in the zucchini and garlic then pour in the stock and season with salt and pepper, keeping in mind that the bacon can be quite salty.

Bring to the boil, reduce the heat, cover and simmer for 5 minutes.

Add the quinoa, cover again and continue to simmer on low heat for another 30 minutes until the quinoa is cooked.

Stir the balsamic vinegar into the soup or, if preferred, everyone can add the vinegar individually into their own soup.

Serve garnished with some torn buffalo mozzarella cheese.

Note *This is a very thick and hearty soup, wonderful on those cold wintry nights, especially if you love mushrooms. You can use any mushroom you like. Also, if you want to add a bit of crunch, sprinkle with some toasted quinoa.*

Wild Mushroom, Zucchini and Thyme Soup

Serves 6–8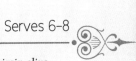

Heat the oil in a large saucepan and sauté onion until soft. Add the mushrooms, zucchini, garlic, thyme leaves, salt and pepper and cook until the vegetables have collapsed. The salt will help do this and draw out all the juices from the mushrooms.

Stir in the lemon zest and pour in the stock. Bring to the boil, reduce the heat and simmer for 30 minutes.

Puree the soup, bring back to the boil, pour in the water and stir in the quinoa. Reduce the heat, cover and simmer for 15–20 minutes until the quinoa is cooked.

Serve with a squeeze of lemon juice and a sprinkle of freshly chopped chives.

2 tablespoons extra virgin olive oil

1 large brown onion, roughly chopped

2 lb 4 oz/1 kg selection of wild mushrooms, roughly chopped and the stalks removed if too woody

1 lb 12 oz/750 g zucchini/courgette, roughly chopped

3 cloves garlic, roughly chopped

2 tablespoons thyme leaves

Salt and freshly ground black pepper

Zest of 1 lemon

8 cups vegetable or chicken stock

1 cup boiling water

⅔ cup quinoa, rinsed and drained

Lemon juice, for serving

Chives or thyme, chopped, for garnish

Note *Black quinoa takes longer to cook than the other varieties so you will have to vary the cooking time according to how tender you would prefer the quinoa to be. You can use whichever quinoa you prefer: I used the black one only because I love the contrast of the black against the vibrant red of the beetroot. Don't forget to wear gloves when peeling the beetroot or you may end up with bright red hands.*

Beetroot, Ginger and Garlic Soup

Serves 6–8

1 tablespoon extra virgin olive oil

2 red onions, chopped

4 large cloves garlic, chopped

1 small knob ginger, grated to make about 1–2 tablespoons

2 lb 4 oz/1 kg fresh beetroot, peeled and chopped

Few sprigs fresh thyme

Zest of 1 lime

Pinch of ground cloves

8 cups hot chicken or vegetable stock

Salt and freshly cracked pepper

⅔ cup black quinoa, rinsed and drained

Lime juice, to serve

Natural Greek yoghurt or sour cream, to serve

Heat the oil in a large saucepan and sauté the onions until soft.

Add the garlic and ginger and cook for about 1–2 minutes until fragrant.

Add the beetroot, thyme, lime zest and cloves and cook for another 2 minutes.

Pour in the stock and season with salt and pepper. Bring to the boil then reduce the heat and simmer for about 40–45 minutes until the beetroot is tender.

Puree the soup, bring back to the boil then add the quinoa, reduce the heat and simmer on low heat, covered for about 20–25 minutes until the quinoa is cooked. Serve garnished with a good squeeze of lime juice and a dollop of yoghurt or sour cream.

Note *For added richness and thickness, stir in some cream just before taking the soup off the heat.*

Shrimp and Corn Chowder

Serves 6–8

Heat the oil in a large saucepan, and sauté onion until soft and slightly golden in colour. Stir in the garlic and cook for 30 seconds.

Add the creamed and frozen corn, chillies and stock, stir, bring to the boil reduce the heat, cover and simmer on low-medium heat for 15 minutes.

Stir in the quinoa, season with salt to taste, bring back to the boil then reduce the heat, cover and simmer for another 15 minutes

Add the shrimp and milk, adjust the seasoning if need be and simmer covered for another 10 minutes.

Switch off the heat, stir in the chives and leave to rest covered for about 10 minutes before serving. The longer the soup is left to rest the more the quinoa will continue to absorb liquid and become thicker.

Serve with a squeeze of lemon or lime juice or stir through the cream, if you wish.

2 tablespoons extra virgin olive oil

1 large onion, chopped

2 cloves garlic, finely chopped

2 x 14 oz/400 g tinned creamed sweet corn

17½ oz/500 g frozen sweet corn kernels

1–2 long green chillies, de-seeded and finely chopped

7 cups chicken stock

⅔ cup red quinoa, rinsed and drained

Salt and pepper

17½ oz/500 g green shrimp/ prawns, peeled and deveined

1 cup milk

3 tablespoons chives, finely chopped

Lemon or lime juice (optional)

Cream (optional)

Salads

Cucumber, Fresh Coconut, Lime and Chilli Salad

Serves 4–6

¾ cup red quinoa, rinsed and
   drained
1½ cups water
4 Lebanese cucumbers, halved and
   sliced diagonally
1 cup freshly grated coconut
1 eschalot/French shallot, finely
   chopped
2 scallions/spring onions, sliced
   diagonally
2 long red chillies, de-seeded and
   chopped

DRESSING
Juice of 2-3 limes
3 teaspoons fish sauce
1 teaspoon sugar
1 tablespoon extra virgin olive oil

Place the quinoa in a small saucepan with the water, bring to the boil, cover, reduce the heat and simmer for 10–13 minutes until the quinoa is cooked and all the water is absorbed. Cool completely.

Place the cucumbers (you can remove the seeds from the cucumber if you prefer, I like to leave them in), coconut, eschalots, scallions and chillies into a large bowl with the quinoa. If you don't mind the extra heat you can leave the seeds in the chillies.

Prepare the dressing by mixing together the lime juice, fish sauce, sugar and oil.

Pour the dressing over the salad and toss really well.

Stand at room temperature for about 30 minutes before serving so that all the flavours combine.

Note *This is my son's favourite salad and he takes it to work two to three times every week. It is filling and satisfying. I often have it in the fridge and everyone uses it as a meal on the run or just as a quick snack.*

Tuna Salad

Serves 4–6

Place the quinoa in a small saucepan with the water, bring to the boil, then reduce the heat, cover and simmer for 10 minutes until all the water is absorbed. Remove from heat and cool completely.

Combine the quinoa with the bell peppers, cucumbers, spring onions, parsley, capers, olives and beans in a bowl and toss well.

Drain the tuna and add to the salad: you can use either tuna in spring water or oil, totally up to you.

Whisk together the vinegar, oil, salt and pepper. Pour over salad and toss through.

1 cup quinoa, rinsed and drained

2 cups water

1 red bell pepper/capsicum, cut into chunks

1 green bell pepper/capsicum, cut into chunks

2 Lebanese cucumbers, diced

6 scallions/spring onions, sliced

3 tablespoons parsley, finely chopped

2–3 tablespons capers, drained

15–20 pitted Kalamata olives, halved

2 x 14 oz/400 g cans cannellini beans, rinsed and drained

1 x 14 oz/400 g can tuna chunks in spring water or oil, drained

DRESSING

1½ tablespoon red wine vinegar

3 tablespons extra virgin olive oil

Salt and freshly ground black pepper

Note This is one of my favourite salads and so colourful. The pomegranate gives it a real jewelled effect, ideal to be used as a Christmas salad.

Pomegranate, Apricot, Pistachio and Pine Nut Salad

Serves 6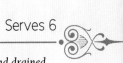

Place the quinoa in a small saucepan with the water, bring to the boil, reduce the heat, cover and simmer for 10 minutes until all the water is absorbed. Remove from the heat and leave to stand covered for at least 10 minutes, then cool completely.

In the meantime, lightly dry roast the pine nuts in a non-stick frying pan until they just start to change colour. Remove from the pan onto another dish so as to cool and stop the cooking process.

Cut the pomegranate in half and using the back of a wooden spoon, bash each half over and into a large bowl to release the fruit and collect the juice.

Add the cooled quinoa into the bowl with the pine nuts, apricots, pistachio nuts and onion.

Mix in the herbs, lemon juice and oil, then season with salt and pepper to taste. Toss well and refrigerate for 30 minutes before serving.

The pistachios can be added just before serving as they can go a little soft if sitting in the dressing for too long.

¾ cup quinoa, rinsed and drained
1½ cups water
3 oz/90 g pine nuts, lightly toasted
1 large pomegranate
5 oz/150 g dried apricots, chopped
5 oz/150 g shelled unsalted pistachios
1 small red onion, finely chopped
½ cup chopped mint
½ cup chopped flat-leaf parsley
Juice of 1 lemon
2 tablespoon extra virgin olive oil
Salt and freshly cracked black pepper

Note *The beautiful vibrant colours in this salad make it ideal to serve for lunch. Here I've paired it with some delicious Herb-crusted Veal Schnitzel (see recipe).*

Bruschetta Salad

Serves 4–6

¾ cup black quinoa grain, rinsed and drained

½ cup white quinoa grain, rinsed and drained

2½ cups water

9 oz/250 g small grape or cherry tomatoes, halved

1 small red onion, finely chopped

1 cup tightly packed fresh basil leaves

2 tablespoons balsamic vinegar

1 tablespoon red wine vinegar

1 small clove garlic, very finely grated

4–5 tablespoons extra virgin olive oil

Salt and freshly ground black pepper

Place the quinoa in a small-medium saucepan with the water. Bring to the boil, reduce the heat, cover and simmer for 12–15 minutes until the quinoa is cooked and all the water is absorbed.

Switch off the heat and stand covered until it cools completely. If the water dries out during the cooking time add a little more. Keep in mind that the white quinoa will cook in less time than the black and will have a softer texture.

Place the cooled quinoa into a bowl with the tomatoes and onion.

Finely chop the basil and stir into the salad. In a separate bowl whisk together the balsamic and red wine vinegar, garlic and olive oil then season well with salt and pepper. Pour over the salad and toss really well.

If possible prepare the salad at least 2 hours before serving as the flavours will blend in and develop more.

Note *This is a delicious salad for a luncheon if you are having guests and you want something a little more special to serve. You can use smoked salmon instead of the trout and for a quick meal at home you can prepare this salad using a good-quality tinned red salmon.*

Smoked Trout and Fennel Salad

Serves 4–6

1 cup quinoa, rinsed and drained

2 cups water

2 small baby fennel bulbs

2 Lebanese cucumbers

9 oz/250 g small cherry or grape tomatoes, left whole

4–6 scallions/spring onions, sliced

½ cup finely chopped dill

14 oz/400 g smoked trout, flaked

Extra dill, chopped, for serving

DRESSING

3 oz/90 g sundried tomatoes

1 teaspoon horseradish (from a jar)

1 small clove garlic, very finely grated

1–2 tablespoons white wine vinegar

4 tablespoons extra virgin olive oil

Salt and white pepper to taste

Place the quinoa in a small saucepan with the water. Bring to the boil, reduce the heat, cover and simmer for 10 minutes until all the water is absorbed. Remove from the heat and leave covered to steam for about 10 minutes.

Trim the fennel bulbs by removing any damaged outer leaves. Then cut in half and slice very finely (baby fennel usually need very little, if any, trimming as they are very young and tender).

Slice the cucumbers in quarters lengthways, then dice and place into a bowl with the fennel, tomatoes, scallions and dill. Add the cooled quinoa and gently toss.

Make the dressing by placing the sundried tomatoes, horseradish, garlic, vinegar and oil into a blender or food processor and process until smooth, then season with salt and pepper.

Pour most of the dressing over the salad and toss with a fork to combine then transfer onto a serving platter.

Drape slices of the trout decoratively over and in the salad, drizzle with the remaining dressing and extra chopped dill before serving.

Note *Use the whole roasted peppers in a jar and slice them yourself as opposed to using ones that are already sliced. I find the ready sliced ones don't drain as well and tend to retain too much of the liquid in the jar, making the salad go soggy.*

Roasted Pepper, Basil and Pine Nut Salad

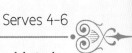

Serves 4-6

Place the quinoa in a small saucepan with the water. Bring to the boil, reduce the heat, cover and simmer for 10 minutes until the quinoa is cooked and all the water is absorbed. Leave to rest covered in the pan for 10 minutes before cooling completely.

Dry roast the pine nuts in non-stick frying pan for a few minutes until they are a pale golden colour. Keep an eye on them as they can burn very easily. Remove from the pan onto to a plate and cool, otherwise they will continue to brown.

Place the quinoa and pine nuts into a large bowl. Add the peppers with the eschalots and basil. Whisk together the olive oil, vinegar and garlic then season with salt and pepper.

Pour over the salad and mix well until all the salad ingredients are coated with the dressing. Transfer onto a serving platter and serve.

Keep some of the pine nuts aside and use scattered over the salad as a garnish or dry roast some extra.

1 cup quinoa, rinsed and drained

2 cups water

4 oz/125 g pine nuts

9 oz/250 g jar roasted bell peppers/
    capsicums, drained and sliced

1 eschalot/French onion, chopped

1 tightly packed cup fresh basil
    leaves, chopped

2–3 tablespoons extra virgin olive
    oil

1–2 tablespoons raspberry red wine
    vinegar or red wine vinegar

1 clove garlic, very finely grated

Salt and freshly cracked pepper

Note *This salad improves the longer it stands when all the flavours have had a chance to be absorbed.*

Bell Pepper, Olive and Garlic Salad

Serves 4–6

Place the quinoa in a small saucepan with the water. Bring to the boil, reduce the heat and simmer, covered, for 10 minutes until the all the water is absorbed. Remove from the heat and leave, covered, for 10–15 minutes to steam. Cool completely.

Core and de-seed the bell peppers then slice into thin matchsticks and place into a deep bowl.

Mix together the vinegar, sugar and chilli flakes and set aside.

Heat the oil in a small frying pan until hot and stir in the garlic. Cook for about 1 minute until it starts to take on some colour.

Remove the pan from the heat and carefully add the vinegar mixture—it will more than likely splatter at this stage so be careful.

Return the pan to the heat for about 30 seconds then pour over the capsicums and toss well. Cover with plastic film and leave to stand until cool.

Add the quinoa, scallions and olives to the bowl with the bell peppers and season with salt and pepper. Check and adjust seasoning and add more vinegar if you think it necessary. Toss the salad well and if possible refrigerate for about 30 minutes before serving.

1 cup quinoa, rinsed and drained

2 cups water

*1 large yellow bell pepper/
   capsicum*

1 large red bell pepper/capsicum

*1 large green bell pepper/
   capsicum*

2 tablespoons brown vinegar

1 teaspoon brown sugar

½–1 teaspoon dried chilli flakes

⅓ cup extra virgin olive oil

3–4 cloves garlic, sliced

*4 scallions/spring onion, finely
   sliced*

*1 cup black pitted Kalamata
   olives*

*Salt and freshly cracked black
   pepper*

Note *This is one of those salads that would be ideal for parties and special occasions. It is so easy to prepare yet looks beautiful when it's dressed and on a platter..*

Prosciutto, Bocconcini and Fig Salad with Herbs

Serves 6

1½ cups quinoa, rinsed and drained

3 cups water

½ cup fresh chives, finely chopped

½ cup mint, finely chopped

5 oz/150 g prosciutto, thinly sliced

7 oz/200 g bocconcini

8 fresh ripe figs

Extra mint, for garnish

DRESSING

1 tablespoon Dijon mustard

1 tablespoon honey

2 tablespoons white or red wine vinegar

⅓ cup extra virgin olive oil

Salt and pepper

Place the quinoa in a small saucepan with the water. Bring to the boil, reduce the heat, cover and simmer for 10 minutes until the quinoa is cooked and all the water is absorbed. Switch off the heat and leave to steam covered in the saucepan for about 10 minutes, then cool completely.

Place quinoa into a large bowl and using a fork lightly toss through the chives and the mint.

Whisk together the mustard, honey, vinegar, olive oil, salt and pepper. Pour ⅔ of the dressing over the quinoa and mix through. Reserve the remainder of the dressing to use just before serving.

When you are ready to serve, place the salad on a serving platter then loosely drape the prosciutto slices on top.

Tear the bocconcini in half and cut the figs into long quarters and arrange around and in the salad.

Sprinkle the top with some extra chopped mint and drizzle with the remaining dressing and an extra twist of freshly cracked pepper.

Note *You can purchase ready-mixed tri-coloured quinoa, which usually consists of the black, red and white quinoa grain. If you can't get it just make up your own by mixing ⅓ cup of each colour or use whatever colour you have at home. As mangoes are seasonal and not always available, this salad is just as delicious without them.*

Honeyed Cashew, Mango and Bean Sprout Salad

Serves 4–6

Place the quinoa in a small saucepan with the water and lime rind, bring to the boil, then reduce the heat, cover, and simmer for 12–15 minutes until all the water is absorbed. Remove from heat and leave to steam, covered, for about 10 minutes then cool completely, remove and discard the rind.

In the meantime, dry roast the cashews in a non-stick frying pan until they start to go a golden colour. Pour in the honey and continue cooking until the honey melts and sticks to the cashews. Keep an eye on them, as you don't want them to burn. Be careful as melted honey can splatter and is very, very hot. Remove from the heat onto a plate to cool.

Combine the quinoa in a bowl with the scallions, bean sprouts, chillies and coriander leaves.

Mix all of the dressing ingredients together and pour over the salad and toss well. Taste and adjust the seasoning and just before serving, toss in the mango and cashews. Transfer to a serving platter and garnish with extra cilantro leaves and slices of chillies.

If you plan to prepare this salad in advance it is best that you add the mango to the salad just before serving, otherwise it can make the salad soggy.

1 cup tri-colour quinoa, rinsed and drained
2¼ cups water
1 large piece lime rind
6 oz/180 g raw cashew nuts
1½ tablespoons honey
4 scallions/spring onions, sliced
2 cups fresh bean sprouts
2–3 long red chillies, deseeded and sliced
½ cup cilantro/coriander leaves, chopped
1–2 large mangoes, peeled and diced
Extra cilantro/coriander leaves, for garnish
Extra sliced chillies, for garnish

DRESSING
Zest of 1 lime
1 clove garlic, finely grated
1–2 tablespoons tamari soy sauce
¼ teaspoon sesame oil
Juice of 2 limes
1 tablespoon extra virgin olive oil
Salt and freshly cracked pepper

Note *This is one of those salads that will keep for quite a few days in the fridge and the flavour only improves every day. I find it very convenient to have this ready for when you are in a hurry and a quick dose of nourishment is required.*

Garbanzo Bean and Cilantro Salad

Serves 4–6

1 cup quinoa, rinsed and drained

2 cups water

1 yellow bell pepper/capsicum

1 red bell pepper/capsicum

1 green bell pepper/capsicum

2 x 7 oz/400 g cans garbanzo
   beans/chickpeas, rinsed and
   drained

1 red onion, finely chopped

1–2 fresh chillies, chopped

½ cup chopped cilantro/coriander
   leaves

DRESSING

4 tablespoons lime juice

1 tablespoon red wine vinegar

4 tablespoons extra virgin olive
   oil

Salt and freshly cracked pepper

Place the quinoa in a small saucepan with the water. Bring to the boil, reduce the heat, cover and simmer for 10 minutes until all the water is absorbed. Remove from the heat and leave covered to steam for about 10 minutes then cool completely.

De-seed and remove the membrane from the bell peppers and dice into small pieces. Place into a large bowl with the cooled quinoa, garbanzo beans and onion.

De-seed the chillies before chopping and adding to the salad or leave the seeds in if you prefer a bit of heat and a bite to the salad. Mix in the cilantro—use as much or as little as you like.

Whisk together the lime juice, red wine vinegar, olive oil and season with salt and pepper then pour over the salad and toss well.

Fennel, Orange and Watercress Salad with Horseradish and Mustard Dressing

Place the quinoa in a small saucepan with the water. Bring to the boil, cover and simmer for 10–13 minutes until the quinoa is cooked and all the water is absorbed. Remove from the heat and leave, covered, to steam for about 10 minutes. Cool completely.

Trim any tough outer leaves from the fennel if necessary, slice in half, remove the core, then slice very finely. Reserve the herby fronds for garnish.

Peel the orange and segment by slicing along either side of each orange segment to release and remove from the outer skin.

Trim the watercress by removing any of the tough stalks and use only the soft leafy parts.

Place quinoa, fennel, orange segments and watercress into a large bowl and gently toss together with your hands.

Whisk together the orange juice with the horseradish, mustard, honey and olive oil, season with salt and pepper.

Pour dressing over salad and gently toss. Transfer the salad to a serving platter and garnish with the green leafy fronds from the fennel.

¾ cup red quinoa, rinsed and drained

1½ cups water

2 bulbs baby fennel

1–2 oranges, peeled and segmented

1 small bunch watercress

DRESSING

Juice of 1 orange

2 tablespoons horseradish (from a jar)

1 tablespoon grain mustard

1 tablespoon honey

2 tablespoons extra virgin olive oil

Salt and freshly ground black pepper

Chicken, Cranberry and Pistachio Salad

Serves 4-6

1 cup quinoa, rinsed and drained

2 cups chicken stock or water

2 skinless chicken breast fillet
  halves

Extra virgin olive oil

Ground sweet paprika

Salt and freshly cracked black
  pepper

4 oz/125 g dried cranberries

3 oz/90 g shelled roasted pistachio
  nuts

3 tablespoons chopped parsley,

3 tablespoons chopped chives

DRESSING

3 tablespoons orange juice

2 tablespoons lemon juice

1 teaspoon English mustard

3 tablespoons extra virgin oil

Salt and freshly cracked black
  pepper

Place the quinoa in a small saucepan with the stock or water. Bring to the boil, reduce the heat, cover and simmer for 10 minutes until all the water is absorbed. Take off the heat and leave to stand, covered, for about 10 minutes before cooling completely.

Preheat oven to 350°F/180°C.

Rub the chicken breasts all over with a little olive oil, sprinkle with paprika and season with salt and pepper. Place on a baking tray and roast in the oven for about 15–20 minutes until cooked. Remove from the oven, cover with foil and allow to rest.

Place the cooled quinoa, cranberries, pistachio nuts, parsley and chives into a large bowl.

Slice the chicken into bite-sized slices and add to the salad.

Whisk together the orange juice, lemon juice, mustard and oil then pour over the salad and season with salt and pepper.

Gently toss the salad to combine and coat the ingredients with the dressing.

Transfer to a serving platter and serve.

Note *This makes a large salad and is great for a crowd. The quinoa adds an extra crunch and texture, especially as I have used the black quinoa, which tends to remain crunchier than the white one.*

Coleslaw

Serves 4–8

1 cup black quinoa, rinsed and
   drained

2 cups water

¼ small white cabbage, trimmed
   and finely shredded

¼ small red cabbage, trimmed and
   finely shredded

2 carrots, coarsely grated

1 red onion, halved and finely
   sliced

2 stalks celery, finely sliced

Salt and freshly cracked pepper

½ cup mayonnaise

2 tablespoons red wine vinegar

2 tablespoons extra virgin olive
   oil

Place the quinoa in a small saucepan with the water, bring to the boil, then reduce the heat, cover and simmer for 10–14 minutes until all the water is absorbed and the quinoa is tender. Remove from the heat and cool completely.

Combine the quinoa, cabbages, carrots, onion and celery in a large bowl and mix really well—your hands are probably the best mixing tool for this salad.

Stir through the mayonnaise, vinegar and olive oil, season with salt and pepper and toss until well coated.

Cover and chill for several hours before serving.

Pineapple, Coconut and Mint Salad

Serves 6–8

Place the quinoa in a small saucepan with the water and bring to the boil. Reduce the heat, cover and simmer on low heat for about 15 minutes until all the water is absorbed. Remove from the heat and leave to stand, covered, for 10–15 minutes then cool completely.

If using fresh pineapple, peel and core pineapple and cut into small bite-sized pieces.

Place the quinoa and pineapple into a bowl with the coconut, scallions mint and chillies

To make the dressing, place the sugar and lime juice into a small bowl and whisk until the sugar dissolves then whisk in the oil and season with salt and pepper, pour over the salad and mix until all the salad ingredients are coated with the dressing.

If possible, cover and refrigerate for about 30 minutes before serving, the longer the better for all the flavours combine even more.

⅔ cup black quinoa

1½ cups water

1 small–medium fresh pineapple or 1 x 28 oz/800 g can diced pineapple, in juice

1 cup shredded coconut

3 scallions/spring onions, finely chopped

½ cup mint leaves, coarsely chopped

2 long red chillies, sliced

DRESSING

1–2 teaspoons sugar (if fresh pineapple is used)

Juice of 1 lime

2 tablespoons extra virgin olive oil

Salt

Pineapple, Coconut and Mint Salad

Serves 6-8

Place the quinoa in a small saucepan with the water and bring to the boil. Reduce the heat, cover and simmer on low heat for about 15 minutes until all the water is absorbed. Remove from the heat and leave to stand, covered, for 10–15 minutes then cool completely.

If using fresh pineapple, peel and core pineapple and cut into small bite-sized pieces.

Place the quinoa and pineapple into a bowl with the coconut, scallions mint and chillies

To make the dressing, place the sugar and lime juice into a small bowl and whisk until the sugar dissolves then whisk in the oil and season with salt and pepper, pour over the salad and mix until all the salad ingredients are coated with the dressing.

If possible, cover and refrigerate for about 30 minutes before serving, the longer the better for all the flavours combine even more.

⅔ cup black quinoa

1½ cups water

1 small–medium fresh pineapple
    or 1 x 28 oz/800 g can diced
    pineapple, in juice

1 cup shredded coconut

3 scallions/spring onions, finely
    chopped

½ cup mint leaves, coarsely
    chopped

2 long red chillies, sliced

DRESSING

1–2 teaspoons sugar (if fresh
    pineapple is used)

Juice of 1 lime

2 tablespoons extra virgin olive
    oil

Salt

Note *This is a really nice dish for a special summer lunch although good anytime of the year. You can omit the prosciutto altogether for a refreshing vegetarian option.*

Papaya with Prosciutto, Tomato, Mint and Chives

Serves 4

⅔ cup white quinoa, rinsed and
  drained

⅓ cup black quinoa, rinsed and
  drained

2 cups water

2 Lebanese cucumbers, cut into
  small pieces

2 tomatoes, cut into small pieces

3 tablespoons mint, chopped

3 tablespoons chives, chopped

6–8 slices prosciutto, cut into thin
  slices

2 small to medium papaya, halved
  and seeded

Slices of limes, for decoration

DRESSING

2 tablespoons extra virgin olive
  oil

Juice and zest of ½ lime

Salt and freshly cracked black
  pepper

Place the quinoa into a small saucepan with the water. Bring to the boil, reduce the heat, cover and simmer for 12–15 minutes until all the water is absorbed. Remove from heat and leave to stand, covered, for 10–15 minutes then cool completely.

When quinoa has completely cooled, place in a bowl with the cucumbers, tomatoes, mint and chives.

To make the dressing, whisk together the oil, lime juice, zest, salt and pepper. Pour over the salad and gently toss, then add the prosciutto slices and gently mix through the salad.

Cut a very thin slice off the bottom of each papaya so that it will sit straight on the plate and remove all the seeds.

Fill each papaya half with the salad.

Note *Toasted quinoa goes particularly well with a quick tossed salad. It adds body, texture and crunch to an otherwise basic dish. The dressing can be stored in the refrigerator in a jar with a lid. Vary the ingredients below to suit your tastes and seasonal produce.*

Avocado Salad with Toasted Quinoa and a Balsamic Vinaigrette Dressing

Serves 4

Prepare the dressing first by whisking the vinegar, mustard, honey, garlic, and salt together until the salt has dissolved.

Slowly add the olive oil, whisking constantly until you have a runny but thick dressing. Stir in the pepper, then taste and adjust the seasoning.

Place all of your salad ingredients in a bowl with a few tablespoons of the dressing and toss well.

Place on to a serving platter and garnish with extra toasted quinoa and serve immediately. Serve the remaining salad dressing in a jug for people to help themselves.

2 avocadoes, peeled and diced

2 small Lebanese cucumbers, sliced

1 red onion, thinly sliced

Selection of mesclun/mixed gourmet salad leaves

9 oz/250 g grape or cherry tomatoes

1 cup toasted quinoa (see recipe)

Extra toasted quinoa, for garnish

DRESSING

¼ cup good balsamic vinegar

2 teaspoons Dijon mustard

2 tablespoons honey

1 clove garlic, very finely grated

Salt

¾ cup extra virgin olive oil

Freshly cracked black pepper

Vegetarian

Mozzarella and Roasted Pepper Stuffed Mushrooms

Serves 4

¾ cup quinoa, rinsed and drained

1½ cups water

12 large mushrooms

1 tablespoon extra virgin olive oil

4 scallions/spring onions, finely chopped

2 cloves garlic, finely chopped

2 tablespoons finely chopped flat-leaf parsley

7 oz/200 g roasted bell peppers/capsicums, chopped

7 oz/200 g mozzarella cheese, cut into small pieces

1 tablespoon grated parmesan cheese plus extra for sprinkling

Salt and freshly cracked black pepper

DRESSING

3 tablespoons extra virgin olive oil

2 tablespoons balsamic vinegar

Salt and freshly cracked black pepper

Place the quinoa in a small saucepan with the water and bring to the boil. Reduce the heat, cover and simmer for 10 minutes until all the water is absorbed and the quinoa is cooked. Cool a little.

Gently wipe over the mushrooms and remove the stalk. Put 8 of the mushrooms aside and finely chop the remaining mushrooms including all of the stalks if they are not too woody or tough.

Preheat oven to 375°F/190°C and line a baking tray with baking parchment/paper.

Heat oil in a non-stick frying pan and sauté the scallions until lightly browned. Add the chopped mushrooms and cook for 3–4 minutes until the mushrooms collapse. Stir in the garlic and parsley and cook for about 1 minute, remove from the heat and cool a little.

When cooled, stir in the quinoa, roasted bell peppers, mozzarella and parmesan cheeses, and season with salt and pepper.

Place mushrooms top side (domed side) down onto the prepared tray and cover the underside of each mushroom with some of the filling squashing it down tightly as you fill it.

Drizzle with a little olive oil and sprinkle with a little extra parmesan cheese. Place in the oven and bake for about 15 minutes until the cheeses have melted.

To make the dressing, mix all the ingredients together.

Drizzle the mushrooms with some of the dressing before serving.

Vegetarian

Note *This is a lovely vegetarian dish that re-heats beautifully. I prefer to add the chillies as a garnish instead of stirring the chillies into the dish. That way any children who don't like chilli can still eat the dish and everyone else gets as much or as little chilli as they like.*

Spinach with Lentils and Pine Nuts

Serves 6

4 oz/125 g pine nuts

1 tablespoon extra virgin olive oil

6 scallions/spring onions, finely
  chopped

2–3 cloves garlic, finely chopped

2 x 14 oz/400 g cans brown lentils,
  rinsed and drained

2 cups quinoa, rinsed and
  drained

4 cups hot vegetable stock

Salt and freshly ground black
  pepper

9 oz/250 g fresh baby spinach
  leaves

Lemon juice, for serving

Natural Greek yoghurt, for
  serving

Red chillies, sliced for garnish
  (optional)

Dry-roast the pine nuts in a small non-stick frying pan until lightly browned. Remove from the pan and set aside. Don't be tempted to leave them in the pan, as they will continue to brown in the residual heat.

Heat oil in a large saucepan and sauté scallions until soft, stir in the garlic and cook for 1–2 minutes.

Add the lentils and quinoa, give the pot a good stir, then pour in the hot stock and season with a little salt and pepper, keeping in mind that stock is normally salty.

Bring to the boil, reduce heat, cover and simmer for 20 minutes until almost all the liquid has been absorbed.

Stir in the spinach, cover and continue simmering on low heat for another 5 minutes.

Using a fork, stir in the pine nuts, cover then remove off the heat and leave for about 10 minutes before serving with a good squeeze of lemon juice and a dollop of yoghurt.

Garnish with a few slices of red chillies.

Sauerkraut

Serves 4–8

2 tablespoons extra virgin olive
  oil
1 large onion, halved and finely
  sliced
3 cups finely shredded red
  cabbage
3 cups finely shredded green
  cabbage
Salt and freshly cracked black
  pepper
¾ cup black quinoa, rinsed and
  drained
2 cups hot vegetable stock
¼ cup red wine vinegar
2–3 tablespoons flat-leaf parsley,
  finely chopped

Heat the oil in a heavy-based saucepan and sauté the onion until soft.

Add the red and green cabbage, season with salt and pepper and stir well. Cook for about 5 minutes on medium heat until the cabbage starts to soften and collapse.

Stir in the quinoa, mix well into the cabbage and onion, then pour in the stock and vinegar.

Bring to the boil, reduce the heat, cover and simmer for about 25–30 minutes until the quinoa is cooked and the cabbage is tender. Add a little extra water during cooking if you feel the mixture is too dry and the quinoa not quite cooked yet.

Stir in the parsley and it is ready to serve. Taste to see if you need to add more vinegar or let everyone add more to their own portion.

You can eat this sauerkraut hot as a side dish to meat, chicken or fish, or as a meal on its own if you like cabbage. Alternatively, serve this cold as a salad.

Lemon, Thyme and Garlic Crumbed Mushrooms

Serves 4

Prepare the mushrooms by gently wiping them and removing the stalks.

Mix together the quinoa flakes, thyme, lemon zest, garlic, salt and pepper.

Place the flour on a plate. Lightly beat the eggs in a bowl. Lightly dust each mushroom with flour, dip into the egg wash then press into the quinoa flake mixture making sure you cover each mushroom completely.

Heat enough oil on medium heat until it is hot to come halfway up the mushrooms and gently fry until golden, about 2 minutes each side.

Drain on absorbent paper and serve on a bed of arugula leaves with a good squeeze of lemon juice.

8 large mushrooms, such as Swiss brown

1½ cups quinoa flakes

1–2 tablespoons finely chopped thyme

Zest of 1 lemon

2 cloves garlic, finely grated

Salt and freshly cracked black pepper

½ cup quinoa flour

3 extra large eggs

Extra virgin olive oil for frying

Arugula/rocket leaves, for serving

Savoury Zucchini, Tomatoes and Black Beans with Basil

Serves 4-6

Heat the oil in a large frying pan, add the tomatoes and toss gently in the oil to slightly cook and blister the skin about 3–4 minutes. Remove from the pan and set aside.

Add the onion and zucchini to the pan and sauté until onions are soft and golden and zucchini lightly browned.

Stir in garlic and quinoa, and season with salt and pepper. Pour in the stock, bring to the boil, reduce the heat, cover and simmer for 15 minutes until all the liquid is absorbed and the quinoa is cooked.

Stir in the spinach and, once it has wilted, return the tomatoes to the pan with the beans and basil and gently mix through.

Simmer, covered, for another 3–5 minutes until the beans and tomatoes are heated through then take off the heat and leave for about 5 minutes before serving.

For an added tang, I like to drizzle some balsamic vinegar over the top before serving.

3 tablespoons extra virgin olive oil

9 oz/250 g small grape or cherry tomatoes

1 large red onion, chopped

3 medium zucchini/courgette, sliced

3 cloves garlic, chopped

1½ cups quinoa, rinsed and drained

Salt and pepper

2½ cups hot vegetable stock or water

7 oz/200 g fresh baby spinach leaves

2 x 14 oz/400 g can black beans, drained

Small handful of fresh basil leaves, thinly sliced

Balsamic vinegar (optional)

Mozzarella and Roasted Pepper Stuffed Mushrooms

Serves 4

¾ cup quinoa, rinsed and drained

1½ cups water

12 large mushrooms

1 tablespoon extra virgin olive oil

4 scallions/spring onions, finely
chopped

2 cloves garlic, finely chopped

2 tablespoons finely chopped flat-
leaf parsley

7 oz/200 g roasted bell peppers/
capsicums, chopped

7 oz/200 g mozzarella cheese, cut
into small pieces

1 tablespoon grated parmesan
cheese plus extra for sprinkling

Salt and freshly cracked black
pepper

DRESSING

3 tablespoons extra virgin olive
oil

2 tablespoons balsamic vinegar

Salt and freshly cracked black
pepper

Place the quinoa in a small saucepan with the water and bring to the boil. Reduce the heat, cover and simmer for 10 minutes until all the water is absorbed and the quinoa is cooked. Cool a little.

Gently wipe over the mushrooms and remove the stalk. Put 8 of the mushrooms aside and finely chop the remaining mushrooms including all of the stalks if they are not too woody or tough.

Preheat oven to 375°F/190°C and line a baking tray with baking parchment/paper.

Heat oil in a non-stick frying pan and sauté the scallions until lightly browned. Add the chopped mushrooms and cook for 3–4 minutes until the mushrooms collapse. Stir in the garlic and parsley and cook for about 1 minute, remove from the heat and cool a little.

When cooled, stir in the quinoa, roasted bell peppers, mozzarella and parmesan cheeses, and season with salt and pepper.

Place mushrooms top side (domed side) down onto the prepared tray and cover the underside of each mushroom with some of the filling squashing it down tightly as you fill it.

Drizzle with a little olive oil and sprinkle with a little extra parmesan cheese. Place in the oven and bake for about 15 minutes until the cheeses have melted.

To make the dressing, mix all the ingredients together.

Drizzle the mushrooms with some of the dressing before serving.

Note *To make this dish vegan, use a non-dairy yoghurt or sour cream. This is also great if you use it as a filling for tacos or burritos. Try it with some guacamole or tomato salsa.*

Chilli Beans

Serves 4

2 tablespoons extra virgin olive oil

1 large red onion, chopped

3 cloves garlic, chopped

2 teaspoons ground sweet paprika

2 teaspoons ground oregano

1½ tablespoons ground cumin

½–1 teaspoon dried chilli flakes

1 x 14 oz/400 g can diced tomatoes

1½ cups quinoa, rinsed and drained

2½ cups boiling water

Pinch of salt

2 x 14 oz/400 g cans red kidney beans, rinsed

½ cup chopped cilantro/coriander leaves

Lime juice

Sour cream or natural Greek yoghurt, for serving

Heat the oil in a large frying pan and sauté onion until soft and golden. Add the garlic and cook for about 30 seconds until fragrant. Stir in the paprika, oregano, cumin and chilli flakes.

Add the tomatoes, and cover and simmer on low heat for about 5 minutes.

Stir in the quinoa, water and salt. Bring to the boil, reduce the heat, cover and simmer for 15 minutes.

Add the beans and cook for another 5–10 minutes until the beans have heated through and the quinoa is cooked.

Stir in the fresh coriander and it is ready to serve with a squeeze of lime juice and a dollop of sour cream or yoghurt.

Note This is a delicious and very nutritional meal. One of my family's favourites.

Eggplant with Kale and Lentils

Serves 4–6

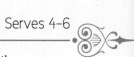

Heat the oil in a large frying pan and cook eggplant until golden brown, remove from the pan. Add the onion to the pan (you may need to add a little more oil as the eggplant tends to absorb oil quite quickly) and continue cooking until onion is soft.

Stir in garlic, ginger, cumin, coriander and chilli, and cook for about 30 seconds.

Stir in the kale and cook for 1–2 minutes until it softens and collapses. (To prepare the kale discard the thick woody stalks then slice the leaves and softer part of the stalks into very thin strips.)

Add the quinoa to the pan with the lentils and water and season with salt. Bring to the boil, reduce the heat, cover and simmer for about 15 minutes. Gently stir in the eggplant and cook for another 5 minutes

Serve with lemon juice or balsamic vinegar sprinkled over.

4 tablespoons olive oil

1 eggplant/aubergine (approximately 24 oz/750 g), cubed

1 large onion, finely chopped

3 cloves garlic, finely chopped

1 tablespoon grated fresh ginger

1½ teaspoons ground cumin powder

1½ teaspoons ground coriander

1 teaspoon chilli flakes

2 cups finely sliced kale

1 cup quinoa, rinsed and drained

2 x 14 oz/400 g can lentils, undrained

1¼ cups hot water

Salt to taste

Lemon juice or balsamic vinegar, for serving

Note These little filled pumpkins are a real conversation piece. For a non-vegetarian option, add some chopped bacon or chorizo with the leek and onion. As an alternative, you can prepare a whole pumpkin instead of little individual ones. You will need to cook the pumpkin for longer until it is soft inside but still firm on the outside. Drain off any liquid that may come out of pumpkin before adding the filling.

Stuffed Nugget Pumpkins Creole

Serves 6

Place the quinoa in a small saucepan with the water. Bring to the boil, reduce the heat, cover and cook for 10–12 minutes until all the water is absorbed. Take off the heat and leave to stand, covered, as you prepare the rest of the dish.

Preheat oven to 325°F/160°C.

Cut a lid off the top of each pumpkin and reserve. Remove all the seeds from the pumpkins and replace the lid.

Place the pumpkins in a baking tray and bake for about 20–30 minutes until pumpkins are not cooked right through but soft on the inside and still firm on the outside. Remove from the oven and cool.

In the meantime prepare the filling: heat the oil with the butter in a large frying pan and cook the onion and leek until soft.

Add the bell peppers, corn and chilli and cook for about 3–5 minute until the peppers are soft and the corn has defrosted.

Stir in the quinoa flour and cook, stirring constantly for about 1–2 minutes just to cook out the raw flour taste and so that the mixture doesn't stick to the pan.

Pour in the milk and stir until the mixture starts to bubble and thicken.

Stir in the cheese and red quinoa grain, and season with salt and pepper. Once the cheese has melted take off the heat.

Fill each pumpkin with the filling, replace the lid and bake for about 20–25 minutes or so until the pumpkins feel soft right through when tested.

⅔ cup red quinoa, rinsed and
  drained
1⅓ cups water
6 small nugget pumpkins,
  about 16 oz/450 g each

FILLING
2 tablespoons extra virgin olive
  oil
1 teaspoon butter
1 large red onion, chopped
1 leek, trimmed, washed and finely
  sliced
½ green bell pepper/capsicum, seeds
  removed and diced
½ red bell pepper/capsicum, seeds
  removed and diced
1 cup frozen corn kernels
Dried chilli flakes, to taste
2 tablespoons quinoa flour
1¾ cups milk
1 cup mild cheese, grated
Salt and freshly cracked pepper

Note *This tart is best eaten on the day it is prepared. Quinoa flour tastes different to normal wheaten flour and can have an earthy aftertaste, which seems to be more noticeable the day after first baking. Also pastry made solely out of quinoa flour will be darker before and after baking. It is always best to re-heat this in the oven.*

Spinach and Goat's Cheese Tart

Serves 4-6

PASTRY

2 cups quinoa flour

1 teaspoon salt

4 oz/125 g very cold butter, cut into pieces

2 extra large egg yolks

Icy cold water

1 egg white, lightly beaten

FILLING

1–2 tablespoons extra virgin olive oil

4 scallions/spring onions, chopped

2 x 9 oz/250 g packets frozen spinach, thawed

1 large clove garlic, finely chopped

4 oz/125 g goat's cheese or feta

2 extra large eggs

1 cup cream

¾ cup milk

Salt and freshly cracked black pepper

Place the flour and salt in a food processor and pulse for a few seconds to aerate the flour, then add the butter piece by piece and pulse until the mixture resembles thick breadcrumbs.

Add the egg yolks, process a few seconds and then, with the motor running, add as much water as needed, a little at a time until the dough comes together and turns into a ball.

Place onto a bench/counter top that has been dusted with quinoa flour and shape into a flat disc. Wrap in plastic wrap and refrigerate for about 1 hour.

Preheat oven to 350°F/180°C and lightly grease a 10 in/25 cm fluted tart tin with a loose base.

Remove the pastry from the fridge and roll out on a floured surface to fit the prepared tin. Gently collect the pastry by rolling around the rolling pin then gently lift it over and onto the tin. The pastry will be quite fragile so you may need to do a little repair work by pushing pastry into place in the tin. Also the pastry may have some little white specs on it after it has rested in the refrigerator, they are nothing to worry about.

Trim any excess pastry then line the tart with a piece of baking parchment/paper and fill with baking weights.

Place the tart tin on a baking tray and place in the oven to bake for 15 minutes, remove from the oven, then slowly and very carefully remove the paper and the weights. Brush the tart with some of the beaten egg white and return to the oven for another 5 minutes (this seals the inside of the tart and avoids any leakage of the custard).

continued on page 100

In the meantime, prepare the filling by heating the oil in a medium-sized frying pan and sauté the scallions until they start to soften and take on some colour. Squeeze as much of the water as possible from the spinach then add to the pan and cook for about 3 minutes. Stir in the garlic and cook for another 1–2 minutes and remove from the heat.

Scatter the spinach over the tart and crumble the cheese on top.

Whisk together the eggs, cream and milk, and season with salt and pepper (keep in mind that the cheese can be salty).

Carefully pour the milk mixture over the spinach and cheese and bake for about 30–35 minutes until the tart is set.

Remove from oven and rest for about 10 minutes before cutting and serving.

Garbanzo Bean and Spinach Pilaf

Serves 4

Place the quinoa in a small saucepan with the stock and bring to the boil. Reduce the heat, cover and simmer for 10 minutes until all the water is absorbed. Leave covered until needed.

While the quinoa is cooking, heat the oil in a large frying pan and sauté onion until soft and golden. Add the garlic and chilli and cook for about 30 seconds.

Stir in the curry powder and the garam masala and cook for a few seconds.

Add the garbanzo beans and the water, and simmer covered for about 5 minutes. Stir in the spinach and cook until it wilts. If using the frozen spinach, you may need to cook it for about 10 minutes and add a little more water.

Stir in the cooked quinoa, lemon juice and season with salt and pepper and mix well to combine. Serve with a dollop of yoghurt.

1½ cups quinoa, rinsed and drained

3 cups vegetable or chicken stock

2 tablespoons olive oil

1 large onion, cut in half and sliced

2 cloves garlic, finely chopped

1 red chilli, de-seeded and chopped

1½–2 teaspoons curry powder

1 teaspoon garam masala

2 x 14 oz/400 g cans garbanzo beans/chickpeas, drained

7 oz/200 g fresh spinach leaves or 9 oz/250 g frozen, thawed

½ cup water

Juice of half a large lemon

Salt and freshly ground black pepper

Natural Greek yoghurt, for serving

Note *This dish is filling as a vegetarian meal on its own or as a side dish with meat, fish or chicken.*

Cardamom, Chilli and Mustard Seed Pilaf

Serves 4–6

Break open the cardamom pods and, using a mortar and pestle, grind the seeds to a fine powder and set aside.

Heat the oil and melt the ghee in a large deep-frying pan, add the mustard seeds and cook until they start to pop then add the onion and cook until soft.

Stir in the ginger and garlic and cook for about 30 seconds.

Add the ground cardamom, cumin and cinnamon.

Mix the saffron strands with the hot water and let them steep for a few seconds then add to the pan with the quinoa.

Stir well and season with salt and pepper. Bring to the boil, cover and simmer on low heat for about 15–20 minutes until all the water is absorbed

Turn off the heat and leave to stand for about 5 minutes then, using a fork, stir through the chillies, cilantro leaves and lime juice.

Serve with lime wedges.

6–8 cardamom pods or about ½–1 teaspoon powdered, according to taste

1 tablespoon olive oil

1 tablespoon ghee

2 teaspoons mustard seeds

1 large onion, halved, thinly sliced

1 tablespoon grated fresh ginger

3 cloves garlic, finely chopped

1 teaspoon ground cumin

½ teaspoon cinnamon

½ teaspoon saffron strands

4 cups hot water

2 cups quinoa, rinsed and drained

Salt and freshly ground black pepper

2 long red chillies, de-seeded and chopped

¾ cup chopped fresh cilantro/ coriander leaves

Juice 1–2 limes

Lime wedges, for serving

Note When buying the tomatoes choose ones that are ripe but firm and will balance and sit upright in a baking dish. If they don't sit upright, cut a paper-thin slice off the bottom of each one and that will help them balance better.

Stuffed Tomatoes

Serves 4–6

12 large tomatoes

1 tablespoon ghee

1 medium brown onion, chopped

4 scallions/spring onions, chopped

2 cloves garlic, finely chopped

2 teaspoons curry powder

1 teaspoon ground turmeric

1 teaspoon ground cumin

¾ cup currants

1¼ cups quinoa, rinsed and drained

2 cups hot water

Salt and freshly cracked black pepper

3 tablespoons chopped cilantro/ coriander

Extra virgin olive oil, for serving

Cut a slice off the top of each tomato to use as a lid. Using a teaspoon, gently scoop out the pulp. Strain the juices from the pulp and chop the fleshy part and reserve. Discard the seeds.

Invert the tomatoes onto some kitchen paper to drain off any excess moisture while you prepare the filling.

Melt the ghee in a large frying pan and sauté onion and scallions until soft and start to change colour. Stir in the garlic and cook for about 30 seconds, then stir in the curry powder, turmeric and cumin, and cook for about 1 minute.

Add the currants, quinoa and water then season well with salt and pepper.

Bring to the boil, reduce the heat, cover and simmer for about 15 minutes until all the water is absorbed. Cool slightly then stir in the cilantro.

Preheat oven to 350°F/180°C.

Fill each tomato with the quinoa mixture, cover with the lids and place in a baking dish. Scatter the reserved tomato pulp around the tomatoes and drizzle the whole dish with extra virgin olive oil.

Bake for 20–25 minutes until the tomatoes are cooked. Don't worry if the tomatoes split a little while cooking.

Note *It is a good idea whenever using fresh turmeric to wear gloves as the colour will stain your hands.*

Leeks with Mustard and Fresh Turmeric

Serves 2-4

2 leeks

2 tablespoons extra virgin olive
   oil

2 large cloves garlic, chopped

2 red chillies, de-seeded and
   chopped

2 tablespoons Dijon mustard

2-3 teaspoons grated fresh turmeric
   or 1 teaspoon powdered

1½ cups quinoa grain, rinsed and
   drained

3¼ cups water

Salt to taste

Juice of ½-1 lemon

Cut the leeks in half and remove the tough outer skin, then wash really well to remove any dirt and grit between the layers.

Finely slice the leeks, including as much of the green part as is usable.

Heat oil in a large saucepan and sauté the leeks until soft and golden.

Stir in the garlic and chillies and cook for about 1 minute. Add the mustard and turmeric and stir well.

Add the quinoa and water and season with salt. Bring to the boil, reduce the heat, then cover and simmer for 15 minutes until all the liquid is absorbed.

Remove from the heat and leave covered for about 10–15 minutes. Squeeze the lemon juice over the quinoa and, using a fork, gently mix and fluff up the grains.

Serve as is or as a side dish with meat, chicken or fish.

Note *This is my version of a traditional Greek dish called* Youvetsi. *My grandchildren can't get enough of it and you can add more vegetables to the mixture as well, including peas, zucchini, spinach or chopped roasted pumpkin. The Greeks usually make it with lamb. If you are going to make it with lamb, cook some lamb chops with the sauce before adding the quinoa.*

Baked Quinoa with Tomatoes and Cinnamon

Preheat the oven to 350°F/180°C.

Heat the oil in a small frying pan until hot and sauté the onion and garlic until soft and golden. Transfer to a deep, ovenproof baking dish (I use a deep 8 in/20 cm round dish).

Add the tomatoes, cinnamon, water, salt and pepper and stir to mix well. Bake for about 25 minutes until sauce is bubbly and thick.

Stir in the quinoa and boiling water, check and adjust seasoning, cover tightly with foil or a lid then return to the oven. Bake for another 30 minutes, stirring once or twice during cooking time, until quinoa is cooked and all the liquid has been absorbed.

Remove from the oven and rest, covered, for 5 minutes while it continues to steam. Stir through the grated parmesan.

Serve with extra grated parmesan sprinkled on top.

2 tablespoons extra virgin olive oil

1 medium onion, coarsely grated

2 cloves garlic, finely grated

1 x 7 oz/400 g can diced tomatoes, undrained

1 heaped teaspoon ground cinnamon

1 cup water

Salt and freshly ground black pepper

1½ cups quinoa, rinsed and drained

2¼ cups boiling water

½ cup parmesan, grated plus extra to serve

Note *This is a quinoa version of risotto. The only difference is that the stock is added all at once and you don't have stir constantly. The other great thing about this recipe is that you don't have to serve it immediately as you do the traditional risotto. That, to me, is an added bonus as we all know how painful it can be to round everyone up to the dinner table at the same time.*

Creamy Leek and Asparagus 'Quinotto'

Serves 4–6

2 tablespoons olive oil

1 tablespoon butter

1 onion, chopped

2 leeks, trimmed, washed and
    thinly sliced

3 cloves garlic, grated

1 cup white quinoa, rinsed and
    drained

1 cup red quinoa, rinsed and
    drained

4½ cups hot vegetable stock

Salt and freshly cracked pepper

3 bunches asparagus, trimmed and
    sliced

2–3 tablespoons cream

1 teaspoon butter, extra

½ cup grated parmesan

Heat the oil and melt the butter in a large saucepan. Add the onion and leeks and sauté until soft. Use as much of the green tender parts of the leeks as you can.

Stir in the garlic and cook for about a minute then add the white and red quinoa with the stock. Season with salt and pepper to taste, keeping in mind that the parmesan cheese and stock, if you are using store-bought, can be salty.

Stir well, bring to the boil, reduce the heat, cover and simmer for about 10 minutes, then stir in the asparagus excluding the tips (these are added toward the end of the cooking time). If you think of it, give the pot a stir once or twice while it is cooking.

Simmer for another 10 minutes then stir in the asparagus tips with the cream and cook for about 5–8 minutes until the quinoa is soft and almost porridgy and nearly all the liquid is absorbed.

Stir in the extra butter and parmesan, and leave to stand covered for about 10 minutes before serving.

'Mac' and Cheese

Serves 6-8

1½ cups quinoa, rinsed and
    drained

3 cups water

9 oz/250 g ricotta, crumbled

1½ cups frozen peas, thawed

Salt and freshly ground black
    pepper

Handful of tasty or mild cheddar
    cheese, grated, extra

Ground sweet paprika, for
    garnish

CHEESE SAUCE

4 oz/125 g butter

1 tablespoon mild English
    mustard

½ cup quinoa flour

5 cups milk

1 cup grated tasty or mild cheddar
    cheese

½ cup grated parmesan

Salt and freshly ground black
    pepper (optional)

Preheat the oven to 400°F/200°C.

Place the quinoa in a saucepan with the water, bring to the boil, reduce heat, cover and simmer for 10 minutes until all the water is absorbed. Cool.

Place the quinoa, ricotta and peas into a large bowl and season with salt and pepper.

To make the sauce, melt the butter, stir in the mustard then stir in the flour and cook for a few seconds until the butter and flour are well incorporated and a roux is formed.

Slowly pour in the milk and whisk continuously until the sauce thickens and starts to bubble. Stir in the cheeses, taste and adjust the seasoning if necessary, and cook until cheese melts.

Pour the white cheese sauce over the quinoa mixture and gently mix to thoroughly combine. Pour into an ovenproof dish, sprinkle with some extra grated cheese and ground paprika and bake for about 30–40 minutes until golden.

Note This is another quinoa version of risotto.

Pumpkin and Spinach 'Quinotto'

Serves 4–6

Preheat the oven to 400°F/200°C and line a baking tray with baking parchment/paper. Place the pumpkin on the tray, lightly coat with a little olive oil and season with salt and pepper.

Bake for 20–30 minutes until the pumpkin is tender and a little charred.

Heat the oil and melt the butter in a large saucepan, then add the onion and sauté until soft. Stir in the garlic and nutmeg and cook for about 30 seconds.

Add the quinoa with the stock, and season with salt and pepper to taste. Keep in mind that the parmesan and stock, if you are using store-bought, can be salty.

Stir well, bring to the boil, reduce the heat, cover and simmer for about 15–20 minutes until all the stock is almost absorbed. If you think of it, and only if you think of it, give the pot a stir once or twice during cooking.

Add the spinach and mix it in with the quinoa until it wilts, cook for 2 minutes then stir in the extra butter, parmesan cheese and the pumpkin.

Take off the heat and leave to stand for about 5–10 minutes until the quinoa is soft and creamy.

2 lb/900 g butternut squash/
*   pumpkin, peeled and cubed*
Olive oil, to drizzle
Salt and freshly cracked black
*   pepper*
1 tablespoon olive oil
1 tablespoon butter
1 large onion, finely chopped
3 cloves garlic, finely grated
¼ teaspoon ground nutmeg
2 cups quinoa, rinsed and
*   drained*
4¼ cups hot vegetable stock
Salt and freshly cracked pepper
7 oz/200 g baby spinach leaves
1 tablespoon butter, extra
½ cup parmesan, grated

Note *This is one of those dishes that is really quick to prepare. You can have it either as a meal on its own or as an accompaniment. You can use frozen corn instead of fresh. There is no need to defrost the corn—just throw it in the pan straight from the freezer. If you use canned corn, stir it in with quinoa at the end.*

Mexican Corn and Chilli

Serves 4

1½ cups tri-colour quinoa, rinsed
   and drained

3 cups water

2–3 tablespoons olive oil

1 large red onion, chopped

1–2 red chillies, sliced

3 cloves garlic, chopped

4 cups sweet corn kernels

1 teaspoon ground allspice

½–¾ cup chopped mint

½–¾ cup chopped cilantro/
   coriander leaves

Juice of 2 limes

Salt

Natural Greek yoghurt or sour
   cream for serving

Chilli powder, for garnish

Place the quinoa in a small saucepan with the water and bring to the boil. Reduce the heat and simmer, covered, for 12–15 minutes until all the water is absorbed. Cover and leave to stand covered while you prepare the rest of the dish.

Heat the oil in a large frying pan and sauté the onion until soft and golden. Stir in the chilli, garlic, corn and allspice, and cook until corn is tender, stirring regularly.

Add the mint, cilantro and lime juice, then season with salt.

Stir in the quinoa and mix well to thoroughly combine.

Serve with a dollop of yoghurt or sour cream and a sprinkle of chilli powder.

Note *This is a really good dish if you are a vegetarian or vegan. Kale is full of antioxident and anti-inflammatory nutrients and when coupled with quinoa this dish becomes a very nutritional meal indeed.*

Kale, Carrot, Mushroom and Tomato Stew

Serves 4-6

Heat the oil in a large saucepan and sauté the onion until soft and golden. Stir in the garlic, tomato concentrate and carrots and cook for about 2–3 minutes. Stir the pan 2–3 times during that time as you want the carrots to caramelise a little but not burn.

Add the mushrooms, tomatoes and water, cover and simmer for 5 minutes.

Stir in the quinoa and season to taste with salt and pepper. Bring to the boil; reduce the heat and cook, covered, for about 20 minutes, stirring every now and then.

In the meantime, wash the kale well and cut into bite-sized pieces. Discard any hard, tough stems.

After 20 minutes of cooking the quinoa, stir in the kale in small batches so that it wilts a little after each addition. Bear in mind that kale does not usually wilt as easily or go as soft as spinach.

Once all the kale has been added, cover and simmer for another 10 minutes or so on low heat or until the kale is as tender as you would like it to be.

Take it off the heat and stir in the vinegar; if possible let it stand covered for another 5–10 minutes before serving. Now you may think that adding the vinegar sounds a bit odd but it does make a difference. Start by adding a small amount then add more if you need to.

2 tablespoons extra virgin olive oil

1 large onion, chopped

3 cloves garlic, chopped

1 tablespoon tomato concentrate/ paste

4 carrots, sliced

10 oz/300 g mushrooms, sliced

1 x 14 oz/400 g diced tomatoes, undrained

2¾ cups hot water

1 cup quinoa rinsed and drained

Salt and freshly cracked black pepper

1 large bunch kale (about 14 oz/400 g) when chopped

1–2 tablespoons red wine vinegar

Note *This vegetable cake is so easy to prepare—just throw everything together and bake it in the oven, just like a quiche. It can be eaten warm or cold so it's a good dish to have in the refrigerator to re-heat when needed. Serve this with a light salad.*

Vegetable Cake

Serves 6

24 oz/750 g eggplant/aubergine, cubed

14 oz/400 g zucchini/courgettes, cubed

10 oz/300 g mushrooms, sliced

2 red onions, halved and sliced

5–6 cloves of garlic, unpeeled

Freshly cracked black pepper

Extra virgin olive oil

1 cup quinoa, rinsed and drained

2 cups water

5 oz/150 g roasted bell peppers/ capsicum cut into strips

3 oz/90 g sundried tomatoes, cut into strips

3 oz/90 g pitted kalamata olives

2 teaspoons dried oregano

½ cup flat-leaf parsley, chopped

Salt and freshly cracked black pepper

6 extra large eggs, lightly beaten

Lemon zest, for garnish

Flat-leaf parsley, chopped, for garnish

Preheat oven to 400°F/200°C and grease a 10 in/25 cm loose bottom, spring-form tin with olive oil and line the bottom with non-stick baking parchment/ paper.

Place the eggplant, zucchini, mushrooms, onions and garlic onto two baking trays. Season with pepper (don't add salt at this stage) drizzle liberally with extra virgin olive oil, give the vegetables a good stir and roast for 20–25 minutes.

In the meantime place the quinoa into a medium saucepan with the water. Bring to the boil, reduce the heat, cover and simmer for 10 minutes until all the water is absorbed. Remove from the heat and leave to stand until you need it.

When the vegetables are ready, remove from the oven and leave to cool for a few minutes. Squeeze the garlic to release the puree and discard the skins.

Place all the vegetables, including the garlic, into a bowl then stir in the quinoa, peppers, tomatoes, olives, oregano and parsley. Season with salt and more pepper, if you like, then gently mix in the eggs.

Pour into the spring-form tin, flatten the top, place on a baking tray and bake for 30–35 minutes until golden and set.

Leave for 10–15 minutes before slicing and serving with a leafy green salad. Garnish with lemon zest and parsley if you want, just before serving.

Meat

Chorizo Sausage with Caramelised Onions and Smoked Paprika

Serves 4

1½ cups quinoa, rinsed and
   drained

3 cups water

4 chorizo sausages, thickly sliced

1 tablespoon extra virgin olive oil

2 large onions, halved then sliced

2 cloves garlic, chopped

½–1 teaspoon chilli flakes

2 teaspoons smoked paprika

1½ cups frozen peas

¼ cup water

Salt and freshly cracked black
   pepper

2 tablespoons chopped parsley, for
   serving

Place the quinoa in a small to medium saucepan with the water, bring to the boil, then reduce the heat, cover and simmer for 10 minutes or until all the water is absorbed. Remove from heat.

Sauté chorizo in a large, non-stick frying pan until lightly browned (there is no need to add any oil to the pan at this stage as the chorizo should render some of its own fat).

Remove the chorizo from pan with a slotted spoon and set aside.

Add the oil to the pan if necessary and cook the onion, stirring regularly until soft and caramelised, for about 5 minutes. Stir in the garlic and chilli flakes and cook for about 30 seconds, then stir in the chilli and paprika.

Add the frozen peas and water, and cook for about 4–5 minutes, stirring frequently until peas have thawed and are just cooked.

Stir in the quinoa and the chorizo sausage, season with salt and pepper, and cook for another 3–4 minutes until heated through. Sprinkle with parsley and serve.

Note *The soufflé can be prepared in advance up to the stage where the egg whites are to be whisked and folded in. However you will have to re-heat the ham and cheese mixture beforehand, otherwise the soufflé will not rise. Cover the mixture with plastic wrap to stop a skin forming until ready to re-heat.*

Ham, Cheese and Dijon Mustard Soufflé

Serves 4

Melt the butter in a frying pan and cook the scallions and ham until the scallions are soft and the ham is lightly browned. Remove from the heat and set aside.

Preheat oven to 375°F/190°C and grease 4 x 1-cup capacity ramekins with butter then sprinkle liberally with grated parmesan cheese.

Melt the extra butter in a saucepan, stir in the flour to form a roux and cook for about 30 seconds stirring constantly.

Gradually stir in milk and continue cooking stirring constantly until thickened. Remove from heat and add the egg yolks one at a time, mix well then stir in the mustard and cheese. Return to the heat and keep stirring until cheese has melted. Season with pepper then gently fold in the ham and scallions (you can add a little salt if you like but keep in mind that the cheese and ham will be salty).

Whisk the egg whites with the pinch of salt until stiff and soft peaks form. Fold one large spoonful of egg whites into the ham mixture to loosen, then fold in the remaining egg whites using a metal spoon.

Spoon the mixture evenly into the ramekins and then run your fingertip around the edge of each dish to separate the soufflé from the rim. This will help the soufflé rise more evenly.

Place the ramekins on a baking tray on the middle shelf of the oven and bake for about 20 minutes, until well risen and just set. Remove from the oven and serve immediately. Try not to open oven door during cooking.

1 tablespoon butter

6 scallions/spring onions, chopped

7 oz/200 g double-smoked ham, chopped

Butter, for ramekins

Parmesan, grated, for ramekins

2½ tablespoons butter, extra

3 tablespoons quinoa flour

1¼ cups hot milk

4 extra large egg yolks,

2 tablespoons Dijon mustard

3 oz/90 g sharp or vintage cheddar cheese, grated

Salt and pepper

5 extra large egg whites

Pinch salt

Barbecue Pork with Asian-style Quinoa

Serves 4

2 cloves garlic, grated

1 tablespoon grated fresh ginger

¼ teaspoon five spice powder

2–3 tablespoons tamari soy sauce

2 tablespoons oil

1 tablespoon honey

2 pork fillets, about 2 lb 4 oz/1kg

ASIAN-STYLE QUINOA

1½ cups quinoa, rinsed and
    drained

3 cups water

1 stick lemongrass, bruised

2 star anise

1 large clove garlic, lightly
    smashed

3–4 slices fresh ginger

2 tablespoons tamari soy sauce

2 red chillies, left whole

2 green chillies, left whole

cilantro/coriander leaves, chopped,
    for garnish

Lime juice, for garnish

Preheat the oven to 350°F/180°C.

Mix together the garlic, ginger, five spice powder, soy sauce, oil and honey. Pour over the pork and leave to marinate for 1–2 hours—the longer the better—then roast in the oven for 20–25 minutes or until cooked to your preference. Remove from the oven, cover with foil and rest for 5–10 minutes.

In the meantime, prepare the quinoa by placing it in a medium-sized saucepan with the water, lemongrass, star anise, garlic, ginger, soy sauce and chillies.

Bring to the boil, reduce the heat, cover, and simmer for 10–12 minutes until all the liquid is absorbed. Remove from the heat and leave to stand, covered, for 10–15 minutes.

Toss the cilantro through the quinoa and serve on a large platter with a good sprinkle of lime juice and with slices of the pork fillets on top.

Note *If you are gluten/wheat intolerant, be aware that some sausages are made with breadcrumbs and/or cereal.*

Spicy Italian Sausages with Peppers and Fennel

Serves 4–6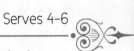

Place the quinoa in a medium-sized saucepan with the water, bring to the boil, cover, reduce the heat and simmer for 10 minutes until all the water is absorbed. Remove from the heat and leave to stand, covered.

Remove the sausage meat from the casings. Discard the casings. Roll the meat into little balls and set aside in the fridge.

Cut the fennel bulbs in half and thickly slice. Reserve any of the green fronds as they will be used to garnish the dish.

Heat the oil in a large frying pan and cook the meatballs until browned and cooked, remove from the pan and put to one side.

Add the onion to the pan and sauté until soft and golden. You may need to add a little more oil.

Add the fennel to the onions with the garlic, peppers, fennel seeds and chilli and cook until the vegetables take on some colour and are tender but still firm.

Return the meat to the pan and season with salt and pepper then stir in the quinoa and lemon juice if using. Gently mix together until the quinoa has combined with all the other ingredients.

Check and adjust the seasoning if necessary and cook on a low heat for about 5 minutes to heat everything through. Garnish with the fennel fronds and serve.

1½ cups quinoa, rinsed and drained

3 cups water

2 lb 4 oz/1 kg spicy Italian sausages

2 bulbs baby fennel

2 tablespoons extra virgin olive oil

1 large onion, halved then sliced

3 cloves garlic, sliced

1 red bell pepper/capsicum, cut into pieces

1 green bell pepper/capsicum, cut into pieces

1 teaspoon fennel seeds

½–1 teaspoon chilli flakes

Salt and freshly cracked pepper

Juice ½–1 lemon (optional)

Note If you are gluten/wheat intolerant, keep in mind that some sausages are made with breadcrumbs and/or cereal. Although this batter will not rise as much as the traditional Yorkshire pudding batter made out of wheaten flour, it is still delicious and gluten/wheat-free.

Toad in the Hole with Brown Onion Gravy

Serves 4

1 tablespoon olive oil

8 thick beef or pork sausages

Sprigs of fresh thyme

BATTER

4 extra large eggs

2 cups full cream milk

1 teaspoon English mustard

Salt

1 cup quinoa flour

1 teaspoon baking powder

1 teaspoon baking soda

BROWN ONION GRAVY

1 tablespoon butter

1 tablespoon extra virgin olive oil

2 large brown onions, halved and
   very thinly sliced

2–3 cloves garlic, grated

2 tablespoons quinoa flour

2–2¼ cups hot beef stock

Good splash tamari soy sauce

1 tablespoon fresh thyme leaves

Salt and freshly ground black
   pepper to taste

Make the batter first by using electric beaters to beat together the eggs, milk, mustard and salt. Add the flour, baking powder and baking soda and continue mixing until you have a smooth batter. Set aside to rest and preheat oven to 450°F/230°C.

Heat the oil in a frying pan until hot and brown the sausages all over. While the sausages are browning, place a deep metal baking dish (about 8 x 10½ x 3 in/20 x 26 x 7 cm) into the oven to heat up until it is really hot.

After browning the sausages, transfer them and any pan drippings into the hot oven dish. Give the batter a quick stir then carefully pour over the sausages and scatter the sprigs of thyme on top.

Bake for 30–35 minutes until the batter is golden and set. Serve immediately with the brown onion gravy.

To make the gravy: melt the butter and heat the oil in a saucepan until hot. Add the onions and sauté until they collapse and are brown in colour but not burnt. Stir in the garlic and cook for another minute. Mix in the flour and stir to form a roux, cook for 1–2 minutes.

Pour in the stock gradually and keep stirring until the gravy thickens. Add the soy sauce, thyme leaves and season with salt and pepper to taste. Cook for 1–2 minutes until you have a smooth and thick gravy.

Chilli Con Carne

Serves 6

Heat the oil in a large, deep frying pan and sauté onion until soft and golden. Add the beef and continue cooking until browned, making sure any lumps are broken up.

Stir in the garlic and cook for about 30 seconds until fragrant, then add the oregano, cumin, paprika and chilli and cook for about 1 minute,

Stir in tomato concentrate then add the undrained tomatoes, salt and water. Reduce heat, cover and simmer on low heat for about 15 minutes.

Stir in the quinoa and boiling water, cover and simmer for about 20 minutes, stirring occasionally until the quinoa is cooked.

Stir in the red kidney beans and simmer on low heat until the beans are heated through and all the flavours have combined (about 5 minutes).

Rest for about 10 minutes before serving with a sprinkling of grated parmesan, some fresh cilantro and a dollop of sour cream. Slices of fresh avocado are also lovely served with this chilli.

2 tablespoons olive oil

1 large onion, finely chopped

17½ oz/500 g ground/minced beef

3 cloves garlic, chopped

2 tablespoons dried oregano

2 tablespoons ground cumin

1 tablespoon ground paprika

½–1 teaspoon chilli powder

2 tablespoons tomato concentrate/paste

2 x 14 oz/400 g cans diced tomatoes

Salt, to taste

1 cup water

1½ cups, quinoa, rinsed and drained

2½ cups boiling water

2 x 14 oz/400 g cans red kidney beans, drained and rinsed

Parmesan, grated, for serving

Cilantro/coriander, chopped, for garnish

Sour cream, for garnish

Avocado, sliced (optional)

Note *Traditionally, Scotch eggs, a favourite Scottish dish, are coated in breadcrumbs and deep-fried. I am not really keen on deep-frying and I find that the method of cooking described here to be just as tasty. These eggs are great when eaten cold, so they are ideal for picnics or for packed lunches.*

Baked Scotch Eggs

Makes 8

8 small eggs

17½ oz/500 g ground/minced beef
  or pork

1 small onion, grated

2 cloves garlic, finely grated

2 teaspoons dried oregano leaves

1 teaspoon celery salt

1 tablespoon olive oil

Freshly ground black pepper

2 cups quinoa flakes

Salt and pepper

1 tablespoon paprika

3 tablespoons quinoa flour

2 extra large eggs, lightly beaten

Extra virgin olive oil, for baking

Place the eggs in a saucepan of water, bring to the boil and cook the eggs for 4–5 minutes only. Remove from the heat and place the pan under cold running water and let the water run over the eggs for 2–3 minutes, then let them sit in the cold water until you are ready to peel them.

Preheat the oven to 375°F/190°C and line a baking tray with non-stick baking parchment/paper.

Place meat in a bowl with the onion, garlic, oregano, celery salt, oil and pepper. Mix together until thoroughly combined.

Divide the meat mixture into 8 portions. Flatten each portion and place a peeled, hard-boiled egg in the centre of each one, then press the mince around it to fully enclose the egg. Repeat this process with the other 7 portions of mince and eggs.

Mix the quinoa flakes and paprika together, then season with salt and pepper.

Dust each meat ball with quinoa flour then coat well and thickly with the beaten egg, then roll in the quinoa flake mixture, gently pressing the mixture into the meat so that they hold together.

Place the eggs on the prepared tray and drizzle with some extra virgin olive oil. Bake for about 25–30 minutes until golden brown. Serve with your favourite sauce or condiment.

Herb-crusted Veal Schnitzel

Serves 4

Lightly pound the steaks with a mallet or rolling pin if the butcher hasn't already done that. If the steaks are too big cut them in half before you start the crumbing process.

Combine quinoa flakes with the chives, parsley, paprika, salt and pepper.

Dust each steak with some flour then dip into the beaten egg, and then press into the flake mixture, making sure the steaks are evenly and well coated.

Heat some olive oil and melt the butter in a large frying pan until hot but not burning hot. The butter adds extra flavour to the oil but you don't have to use it if you don't want to.

When oil is ready, shallow-fry the steaks without over-crowding the pan until golden and crisp, about 2–3 minutes on each side. Drain on kitchen paper.

Serve with lemon juice squeezed on top or with your favourite sauce. A sweet chilli sauce or a delicious relish is always nice served with this schnitzel. Try serving this with some Bruschetta Salad (see recipe).

4 thin veal steaks, about 17½ oz/500 g

1½ cups quinoa flakes

1 tablespoon chives, finely chopped

1 tablespoon parsley, finely chopped

1 teaspoon sweet paprika

Salt and freshly cracked black pepper

⅓ cup quinoa flour

2 extra large eggs, lightly beaten

Extra virgin olive oil for frying

1 tablespoon butter (optional)

Note *When using any Asian sauces or pastes, such as the black bean paste, and soy and oyster sauce, always check the ingredients, as some ingredients used may be derived from wheat products and therefore contain wheat and gluten.*

Beef with Black Bean Sauce

Serves 4

1½ cups quinoa, rinsed and drained

3 cups chicken stock

2 star anise

1 lb 12½ oz/750 g rump or fillet steak, sliced into thin strips

1 tablespoon quinoa flour

2 tablespoons soy sauce

2–3 tablespoons oil

Oil, extra

1 red bell pepper/capsicum, cut into strips

1 green bell pepper/capsicum, cut into strips

6 scallions/spring onion, sliced into 1 in/2.5 cm pieces

3 cloves garlic, finely chopped

2–3 tablespoons black bean paste

1 tablespoon oyster sauce

½–¾ cup water

Place the quinoa in a small saucepan with the stock and star anise, bring to the boil, then reduce the heat, cover and simmer for 10–12 minutes until all the stock is absorbed. Remove from heat and keep warm.

Meanwhile, combine the steak in a bowl with the flour and the soy sauce.

Heat oil until really hot in a wok or a large frying pan, add the meat and any juices from the bowl and cook on high heat until browned, stirring regularly. Remove from wok.

Heat a little more oil in wok; add the bell peppers and sauté on high heat for about 2–3 minutes. Then add the scallions and garlic and sauté for another 1–2 minutes.

Stir in the black bean paste and oyster sauce. Return the meat to the wok with any of its juices and toss well to combine. Pour in the water and keep tossing constantly until mixture starts to boil and thicken.

Rest for about 5 minutes before serving with the quinoa. Remove and discard the star anise from the quinoa before serving.

Note *For added flavour you can toss any leftover flakes and a little of the oil from the pan that you cooked the steak in through the quinoa.*

Spicy Beef with Beans and Quinoa

Serves 4

Place the steak into a bowl with the oil, garlic, tomato concentrate, paprika, cumin, coriander, oregano, chilli and salt. Rub all the spices into the meat so as to completely cover and leave to marinate for at least 30 minutes.

Place the quinoa in a medium to large-sized saucepan with the water. Bring to the boil, reduce the heat, cover and simmer for 5 minutes. Add the beans and continue to simmer for another 5–7 minutes until all the water is absorbed.

Stir in the scallions, cilantro, lime zest and juice to taste, season with salt and pepper, cover and leave to stand while you cook the steak.

Toss the flakes into the marinated meat and mix really well so as to completely cover the meat.

Heat a little oil in a large non-stick frying pan and quickly shallow-fry the steak, until cooked; about 3 minutes each side. This is best done in two lots. Don't worry about it if any of the flakes come off the steak during cooking, these can be used later.

Check and adjust the seasoning in the quinoa and beans, and serve as is with the steak and a dollop of yoghurt.

Squeeze lime juice over the whole dish before serving.

2 lb 4 oz/1 kg rump steak, cut into long thick strips

1 tablespoon extra virgin olive oil plus extra

3 cloves garlic, finely grated

1 tablespoon tomato concentrate/paste

2 teaspoons smoked paprika

2 teaspoons ground cumin

1 teaspoon ground coriander

1 teaspoon ground oregano

Dried chilli flakes, to taste

Salt

1½ cups quinoa, rinsed and drained

3 cups water

1x 14 oz/400 g can red kidney beans, drained and rinsed

4 scallions/spring onions, sliced

3 tablespoons chopped cilantro/coriander

Lime zest and juice

Salt and freshly cracked pepper

½ cup quinoa flakes

Natural Greek yoghurt, for serving

Extra lime juice, for serving

Stuffed Peppers

Serves 6

2 tablespoons extra virgin olive
  oil

1 large onion, finely chopped

17½ oz/500 g ground/minced
  beef

1 tablespoon cumin seeds

2 cloves garlic, finely chopped

1 large fresh tomato, grated

1¼ cup quinoa, rinsed and
  drained

2 cups water

Salt and freshly ground black
  pepper

6 medium-large red or green bell
  peppers/capsicums

Extra virgin olive oil, for baking

Salt and freshly ground black
  pepper, to taste

Handful flat-leaf parsley, chopped,
  to serve

Heat the oil in a large frying pan and sauté the onion until soft and golden.

Add the beef, stir well and cook until lightly browned all over.

Stir in the cumin seeds and garlic and cook for about 1–2 minutes until fragrant.

Add the tomato, quinoa, water and season with salt and pepper, bring to the boil, reduce the heat, cover and simmer for about 10 minutes or until all the water is absorbed. Stir the pan every now and then during the cooking time.

In the meantime, prepare the peppers. Preheat oven to 400°F/200°C.

Cut the peppers in half lengthways then carefully remove all the seeds and membrane from inside.

Alternatively, you can cut a slice off the top of the bell peppers from the stalk end to make a lid then carefully remove all the seeds and membrane from inside.

Fill the bell peppers with the meat filling and place into a baking dish. Cover with their lid if you have cut the bell peppers that way, drizzle with extra virgin olive oil and season with salt and pepper.

Bake for about 20–30 minutes until the capsicums are slightly charred and cooked. Decorate with chopped parsley, just before serving.

Note *I have allowed three cutlets per person but you may want to prepare a few extra. I always find that when I serve these they just tend to disappear and everyone always wants seconds.*

Spiced Moroccan Lamb Cutlets

Serves 4

12 lamb cutlets

1 cup quinoa flakes

1 teaspoon ground cumin

1 teaspoon cumin seeds

½ teaspoon ground coriander

1 teaspoon ground paprika

¼ teaspoon ground cinnamon

½–1 teaspoon chilli flakes

Salt

2 tablespoons Toasted Quinoa (see recipe)

Zest of 1 lemon

3 cloves garlic, finely grated

3 tablespoons flat-leaf parsley, chopped

½ cup quinoa flour

2 eggs, lightly beaten

Olive oil, for cooking

Lemon wedges, for serving

Trim the cutlets and gently pound to thin out just a little and set aside.

Mix together the flakes, ground cumin and seeds, ground coriander, paprika, cinnamon, chilli, salt and toasted quinoa.

Rub in the lemon zest, garlic and parsley and mix well.

Dust the lamb culets with the quinoa flour then dip into the egg, coating well.

Press firmly into the flake mixture, making sure the cutlets are evenly coated.

Heat some oil in a large pan and shallow-fry the cutlets until the coating is crispy and golden, about 3 minutes each side.

Serve with lemon wedges.

Sage-crumbed Pork Cutlets with Apple Sauce

Using a meat mallet or rolling pin, pound the pork cutlets until they are about ½ in/1 cm thick.

Combine the quinoa flakes with the sage, chives and paprika, and season with salt and pepper.

Whisk the eggs with the milk and mustard.

Dust the chops with the flour, dip into the egg then press into the flake mixture to coat evenly. If time permits, rest meat after coating in the refrigerator for 30 minutes or so.

Heat the oil in a large frying pan and shallow-fry the cutlets until golden and cooked on both sides.

To make the apple sauce, place the apples, sugar and water in a small saucepan and bring to the boil. Reduce heat and simmer, covered, until apples are soft. Mash with a fork. If the apples dry out before they are cooked, add a little more water.

Serve cutlets with sauce.

4 pork cutlets

1½ cups quinoa flakes

1½–2 tablespoons finely chopped sage

2 tablespoons finely chopped chives

1 teaspoon ground sweet paprika

Salt and freshly cracked black pepper

2 eggs

1 tablespoon milk

1 tablespoon English mustard

½ cup quinoa flour

Olive oil

APPLE SAUCE

2 green apples, peeled, cored and cut into chunks

1–2 tablespoons brown sugar

½ cup water

Poultry

Note *How much chilli you add to this marinade is really up to you—you can add one, two or even 10, it just depends on how much you like the heat. I find the beautiful, sweet and juicy kernels of the pomegranate cut through the heat of the chillies.*

Piri Piri Chicken with Pomegranate and Herbed Quinoa

Serves 4

8 chicken thigh cutlets/chops

2–4 birds eye chillies, roughly chopped

1 large red onion, roughly chopped

4 large cloves garlic

2 teaspoons garlic salt

2 fresh or dried bay leaves, chopped

2 tablespoons smoked paprika

2 tablespoons Scotch whisky

2 tablespoons Worcestershire sauce

Zest and juice of 2 lemons

1 tablespoon extra virgin olive oil

POMEGRANATE & HERBED QUINOA

1 tablespoon extra virgin olive oil

2 eschalots/French onions, finely chopped

1½ cups black quinoa, rinsed and drained

3 cups hot chicken stock

2 tablespoons chopped thyme leaves

1 large pomegranate

½ cup chopped flat-leaf parsley

Make two or three cuts across the chicken pieces and place in a baking dish.

Place all remaining ingredients into a food processor or blender and process to a fine liquid paste.

Pour over the chicken and rub in, then allow to marinate in the refrigerator for at least 30 minutes—longer, if possible.

Preheat the oven to 375°F/190°C and bake the chicken pieces in the marinade for 35–40 minutes until cooked and golden. Baste with pan juices every now and then during cooking time.

Meanwhile, prepare the quinoa. Heat the oil in a pan and sauté the eschalots until they soften and start to change colour.

Add the quinoa to the pan with the hot stock and the thyme. Bring to the boil, reduce the heat and simmer for about 20 minutes or so until the quinoa is cooked and all the liquid is absorbed. Switch off the heat and leave to steam, covered, for about 10 minutes.

Cut the pomegranate in two. Using a wooden spoon, hit the back of the cut fruit over a bowl, until all the fruit and juices have been released.

Stir the pomegranate seeds and juices and the parsley through the quinoa with a fork and place onto a serving platter.

Serve the chicken on top of the quinoa with a good squeeze of lemon juice.

Note *This is one of those quick and really easy-to-prepare meals that are perfect for dinner after work or for when unexpected guests drop by.*

Spanish Chicken

Serves 4

Rub the chicken with the paprika until well coated. Heat the oil and melt ghee in a large, deep frying pan and brown the chicken all over on medium-high heat until almost half-cooked and a deep golden colour. Remove from the pan and keep warm by covering with foil.

Add the onion to the pan and cook until soft. Stir in the garlic and cook until fragrant.

Lightly crush the saffron and add to the pan with the lemon zest, and season with salt and pepper.

Add the quinoa and stock, stirring everything together well, then return the chicken pieces to the pan and nestle in with the quinoa.

Bring to the boil, reduce the heat, cover and simmer for about 10 minutes. Scatter the olives over the chicken, cover and simmer for another 5–8 minutes until all the liquid is absorbed. Take off the heat and leave to stand for 5–10 minutes.

Sprinkle with the parsley and lemon juice and serve.

2 lb 4 oz/1 kg chicken thigh fillets, skin removed

½–1 teaspoon smoked paprika

1 tablespoon extra virgin olive oil

1 tablespoon ghee

1 large onion, chopped

3 cloves garlic, finely chopped

½ teaspoon saffron strands

Zest of 1 lemon

1½ cups quinoa, rinsed and drained

Salt and pepper

3 cups hot chicken stock

1 cup stuffed green olives

½ cup chopped flat-leaf parsley

Lemon juice

Spicy Chicken with Herbed Quinoa

4 chicken breast fillets

2 teaspoons ground cumin

2 teaspoons ground coriander

1 teaspoon ground turmeric

2–3 cloves garlic, finely grated

1 tablespoon extra virgin olive oil

Juice and zest of 1 lemon

Salt and freshly cracked pepper

1½ cups quinoa, rinsed and
    drained

3 cups water

2 Lebanese cucumbers, cubed

1 red onion, finely chopped

4 scallions/spring onions, sliced

½ cup chopped cilantro/coriander

½ cup chopped mint

½ cup chopped flat-leaf parsley

Juice of 1–1½ lemons, extra

3–4 tablespoons extra virgin
    olive oil

Salt and freshly cracked pepper

Extra cilantro/coriander leaves, to
    garnish

Combine the chicken, cumin, ground coriander, turmeric, garlic, olive oil, lemon juice and zest, season with salt and pepper, and leave to marinate for at least 30 minutes.

Place the quinoa into a medium saucepan with the water. Bring to the boil, reduce the heat and simmer, covered, for about 10 minutes until all the water is absorbed. Remove from the heat and leave to stand, covered, until you need it.

Cook the chicken by grilling, lightly pan-frying or baking in the oven. Once it is cooked, cover with foil and rest for about 10 minutes before serving.

While the chicken is cooking, mix together the quinoa, cucumber, onion, scallions, cilantro leaves, mint and parsley.

Whisk together the lemon juice, olive oil and salt and pepper, and toss through the quinoa.

Slice the chicken and serve with the herbed quinoa. Garnish with extra cilantro leaves and wedges of lemon.

Note Use as many or as few chillies as you like and either leave the seeds in or remove them or do half with seeds in half without—it is entirely up to your own personal taste.

Chilli and Garlic Chicken

Serves 6.

Place the quinoa in a saucepan with the stock or water. Bring to the boil, reduce the heat, cover and simmer for 10–12 minutes until all the water is absorbed. Remove from the heat and leave to stand, covered, while you prepare the chicken.

Coat the chicken with the paprika and 1 tablespoon of oil and season with a little salt.

Heat the extra oil in a large, deep-frying pan and, when the oil is hot, cook the chicken until golden and cooked through on both sides. Remove from the pan and keep warm.

In the same pan, add a little extra oil if needed and sauté the garlic, scallions, chillies and sugar snap peas for 2–3 minutes on medium-high heat stirring constantly until they soften and take on some colour.

Pour in the wine and deglaze the pan, cook for about 1 minute until the alcohol evaporates, then stir in as much zest and lime juice as you like and season with salt to taste.

Add the quinoa and chicken to the pan and gently toss everything together. Cook on low heat for 1–2 minutes until heated through. Serve with wedges of lime.

1½ cups quinoa, rinsed and drained

3 chicken stock or water

2 lb 4 oz/1 kg chicken thigh fillets, trimmed and cut into thickish slices

1 tablespoon paprika

1 tablespoon extra virgin olive oil

Salt

2–3 tablespoons extra virgin olive oil, extra

4–5 large cloves garlic, finely chopped

8 scallions/spring onions, sliced diagonally into large pieces

6–8 long red chillies, sliced (see note)

5 oz/150 g sugar snap peas, string removed

¾ cup white wine

Zest and juice of 1–2 limes

Salt, extra

Note Fresh pasta dough can be easily and successfully made with quinoa flour. The quinoa pasta is a little more delicate to handle than wheaten pasta and requires more patience when making and rolling, especially when making it for the first time. But persevere—it is really worth it. The pasta does not take very long to cook at all and can be a little darker in colour once cooked.

Fettuccini with Chicken and Mushroom Sauce

Serves 4

To make the pasta dough, place all the pasta ingredients in a food processor and process until all the ingredients come together into a ball. At some point, it may seem to you that the processor is going forever and nothing is happening but be patient—the pasta will eventually come together. No need to rest the dough in the refrigerator before shaping.

Use a pasta machine to roll the dough out into fettuccini or your favourite pasta shape.

Heat oil in a large, deep frying pan and brown chicken all over. Set chicken aside.

Add the scallions and garlic to the pan and cook for about a minute. Stir in the mushrooms and continue cooking until mushrooms have collapsed and are soft, about 5 minutes.

Add the cream, stock and nutmeg, stir well, bring to the boil then return the chicken to the pan and season with salt and pepper. Cook, covered, on medium heat for about 8–10 minutes until chicken is cooked and the sauce has thickened.

Cook the pasta in boiling salted water; fresh quinoa pasta only takes about 3–5 minutes to cook once the water comes back to the boil.

Drain and throw the pasta into the pan with the chicken. Toss well, sprinkle with some grated parmesan or romano cheese and serve.

3 tablespoons extra virgin olive oil

26 oz/750 g chicken fillet, cut into strips

4 scallions/spring onions, sliced

4 cloves garlic, finely chopped

14 oz/400 g mushrooms, thinly sliced

10 oz/300 ml cream

¾ cup chicken stock

½–¾ teaspoon ground nutmeg

Salt and freshly cracked pepper

Grated parmesan or romano cheese, to serve

PASTA DOUGH

17½ oz/500 g quinoa flour

½ teaspoon salt

5 extra large eggs

1 tablespoon olive oil

Note This chicken loaf is great for picnics—it is as delicious served cold as it is served warm.

Chicken and Vegetable Loaf

Serves 4-6

17½ oz/500 g ground/minced
    chicken

1 large red onion, finely chopped

2 cloves garlic, finely chopped

2 tablespoons finely chopped
    parsley

2 tablespoons fresh thyme leaves

2 heaped tablespoons horseradish
    (from a jar)

½–1 red bell pepper/capsicum

1 cup frozen peas, thawed

1 cup quinoa flakes

1 tablespoon olive oil

2 eggs

Salt and freshly cracked pepper

Preheat the oven to 400°F/200°C and lightly oil a 10 in/25 cm non-stick loaf tin.

Place ground chicken in a large bowl and add the onion, garlic, parsley, thyme and horseradish, and mix.

Cut the bell pepper in half, remove the seeds and membrane, and cut into very small pieces.

Drain the peas of any water after thawing and add capsicum and peas to the mince.

Stir the quinoa flakes, oil and eggs and season with salt and pepper into the chicken mixture.

Mix really well to thoroughly combine.

Place mince mixture into the prepared loaf tin and bake for 45–50 minutes until golden brown on top.

Remove from the oven, cover with foil and rest for 5–10 minutes before turning out on to a serving platter.

Slice and serve with your favourite chutney or sauce.

Chicken with Bacon, Sage and Onion Stuffing

Preheat the oven to 375°F/190°C.

Heat the oil in a large frying pan and sauté onion and bacon until soft and golden, stir in the garlic and take off the heat. Cool slightly.

Place the bacon, onion and garlic into a bowl with the quinoa flakes, sage, chives, parsley and lemon zest.

Season with salt and pepper. Add the egg then mix together to thoroughly combine. Mixture should be moist and hold together.

Remove any excess fat from the chicken, rinse and pat dry with kitchen paper.

Place the stuffing mixture into the cavity of the chicken and secure the opening with a small metal skewer.

Place the chicken into a baking dish and drizzle with some extra virgin olive oil and a good squeeze of lemon juice. Season the chicken with a little salt and pepper and sprinkle with ground paprika.

Bake for 1 hour 10 minutes to 1 hour and 20 minutes, until the chicken is cooked and a deep golden brown. Baste chicken every now and then with pan juices.

Chicken is cooked when tested with a metal skewer in the thick thigh area and the juices run clear. Cover with foil and allow to rest for 10–15 minutes before serving.

1–2 tablespoons extra virgin olive oil

1 large onion, finely chopped

2–3 rashers bacon, rind removed and chopped

2 cloves garlic, finely chopped

1 cup quinoa flakes

2 tablespoons chopped sage leaves

1½ tablespoons chopped chives

2 tablespoons chopped fresh flat-leaf parsley

Zest of 1 lemon

Salt and freshly cracked black pepper

1 extra large egg

1 whole chicken (about 4 lb/1.8 kg)

Lemon juice

Sweet paprika

Note *This stuffing mixture is really lovely to use and is ideal as a stuffing for the Christmas turkey.*

Chicken Breasts with Cranberries, Orange and Pistachio

 Serves 4

1 tablespoon olive oil

1 red onion, finely chopped

2–3 cloves garlic, finely chopped

1½ cups quinoa flakes

1 tablespoon chopped chives

1 tablespoon chopped thyme

2 oz/60 g shelled pistachio nuts, chopped

2 oz/60 g dried cranberries

Juice and rind of 1 orange

Salt and freshly cracked black pepper

1 extra large egg

4 chicken breast fillets, with skin on

Lemon juice

Olive oil, extra

Sweet paprika

Preheat oven to 350°F/180°C and line a baking tray with non-stick baking parchment/paper.

Heat the oil in a frying pan and sauté the onion until soft, stir in garlic and cook for about 1 minute. Remove from the heat.

Place the quinoa flakes into a bowl with the chives, thyme and pistachio nuts and cranberries.

Stir the orange juice and rind into the onion and garlic mixture, and season with salt and pepper. Add the egg and mix thoroughly.

With your fingers, gently separate some of the skin from the fillet to make a pocket.

Divide stuffing mixture equally between fillets and spread into each pocket. Ensure the filling is completely covered by the skin.

Place the chicken breasts on the baking tray, skin side up. Squeeze lemon juice on top, drizzle with a little extra olive oil, season with salt and pepper and sprinkle with a little paprika.

Bake for 20–30 minutes until chicken is cooked and skin golden. Remove from the oven and cover with foil to rest for about 10 minutes before serving.

Note *Black cardamom has a smoky flavour—you can use the green variety if you prefer.*

Roasted Quail with Black Cardamon and Curry Leaf Quinoa

Serves 4

1½ cups quinoa, rinsed and
   drained

3 cups hot chicken stock

4 tablespoons quinoa flakes

2 tablespoons fresh thyme leaves

2 tablespoons extra virgin olive
   oil

2 tablespoons honey

2 tablespoons lime or lemon juice

8 quails

Salt and pepper

2 tablespoons extra virgin olive oil,
   extra

6–8 black cardamom pods

1 knob ginger, sliced

4 cloves garlic, sliced

Small handful fresh curry leaves

Long dried chillies, left whole

Salt

½ cup chopped fresh cilantro/
   coriander

Lime juice

Place the quinoa in a medium saucepan with the stock. Bring to the boil, reduce the heat, cover and simmer for 10 minutes until all the water is absorbed. Take off the heat and leave to stand, covered, until you need it.

Preheat the oven to 350°F/180°C. Combine the flakes and thyme leaves and set aside.

Whisk together the oil, honey and lime or lemon juice.

Rinse the quails, remove any feathers and pat dry with kitchen paper. Tie the ends of the drumsticks together with kitchen string and push the tip of the wing behind the breast. Season with salt and pepper, then brush the quails generously with the honey mixture.

Sprinkle the flakes liberally all over the quails gently pressing them on, and then drizzle the rest of the honey mixture on top.

Place on a baking tray and roast for 20–30 minutes until golden and cooked, remove from the oven, cover with foil and keep warm.

Heat the extra oil in a large frying pan. Lightly crush the cardamom pods and throw them into the pan with the ginger, garlic, curry leaves and as many chillies as you like. Stir and cook for about 1–2 minutes until fragrant.

Stir in the quinoa, season with salt and continue cooking until the quinoa is heated through. Toss in the cilantro then serve on a large platter with the quails on top and lime juice squeezed over.

Note *Chicken thigh cutlets are also known as chicken chops and are the thigh with just one main thick bone left in them. They are great for use in dishes such as this one or in casseroles and curries, as the thigh meat can take longer cooking time and the bone adds more flavour. You can use breast meat, drumsticks, whole chicken legs with a portion of the backbone attached, or wings if you prefer.*

Baked 'Fried' Chicken

Serves 3–6

6 chicken thigh cutlets/chops, with skin on

1 cup buttermilk

Salt and freshly ground black pepper

Lemon juice, for serving

COATING

1 cup quinoa flour

1 teaspoon smoked paprika

1 teaspoon sweet paprika

1 teaspoon celery salt

1 teaspoon ground turmeric

½ teaspoon chilli powder

Finely grated zest of 1 lemon

Drizzle of olive oil

Lemon juice, to serve

Buy even-sized chicken pieces. Make three incisions along each cutlet, cutting through the skin and a bit of the meat part.

Place into a bowl with the buttermilk and a little salt and pepper. Coat well, making sure you rub the buttermilk into each incision and the chicken is completely covered with it.

Leave to marinate in the fridge for at least 2–4 hours. The longer the better—even overnight is fine.

Preheat the oven to 400°F/200°C and line a baking tray with non-stick baking parchment/paper.

Make the coating by mixing the quinoa flour with the smoked and sweet paprika, celery salt, turmeric, chilli and lemon zest. Make sure all the spices are evenly distributed through the flour.

Give the chicken a little shake to remove any excess buttermilk, as you don't want it dripping in liquid, then coat completely with the coating mixture.

Place the chicken on the baking tray and drizzle very lightly with a little olive oil, place in the oven and bake for 40–50 minutes until the chicken is cooked and golden brown.

Rest for 5 minutes, loosely covered in foil, before serving with a squeeze of lemon juice. Delicious!

Mushroom, Bacon and Thyme-stuffed Chicken Breasts

Serves 4

Preheat the oven to 350°F/180°C.

Heat the oil in a non-stick frying pan and sauté bacon until golden. Add the mushrooms and scallions, and continue cooking until mushrooms are soft (you may need to add a little more oil if the pan becomes too dry).

Add the garlic and cook for a few seconds until fragrant then stir in the mustard and season with salt and pepper, keeping in mind the saltiness of the bacon.

Mix in the quinoa then remove from the heat and allow to cool a little.

Meanwhile, trim the chicken breast of any fat or sinews and cut a deep pocket along the length of each breast without cutting right through.

When the mushroom mixture is just warm, add the egg and mix well to thoroughly combine.

Fill each chicken breast with the mushroom mixture then secure the opening with a metal skewer.

Place the chicken on a baking dish and drizzle with a little olive oil. Spread each one with some Dijon mustard and a good sprinkle of thyme leaves.

Season with salt and pepper and bake for 20–25 minutes until golden and the chicken is cooked. Remove from the oven, cover and rest for about 5 minutes before serving.

1 tablespoon extra virgin olive oil

5 oz/150 g bacon, diced

5 oz/150 g mushrooms, diced

4 scallions/spring onions, finely chopped

2 cloves garlic, finely chopped

1 tablespoon Dijon mustard

Salt and freshly cracked black pepper

1 cup quinoa flakes

1 extra large egg

4 chicken breast fillets

Extra virgin olive oil

1 tablespoon Dijon mustard, extra

Thyme leaves, extra

Salt and freshly cracked black pepper, extra

Note Black cardamom has a smoky flavour—you can use the green variety if you prefer.

Roasted Quail with Black Cardamon and Curry Leaf Quinoa

 Serves 4

1½ cups quinoa, rinsed and drained

3 cups hot chicken stock

4 tablespoons quinoa flakes

2 tablespoons fresh thyme leaves

2 tablespoons extra virgin olive oil

2 tablespoons honey

2 tablespoons lime or lemon juice

8 quails

Salt and pepper

2 tablespoons extra virgin olive oil, extra

6–8 black cardamom pods

1 knob ginger, sliced

4 cloves garlic, sliced

Small handful fresh curry leaves

Long dried chillies, left whole

Salt

½ cup chopped fresh cilantro/ coriander

Lime juice

Place the quinoa in a medium saucepan with the stock. Bring to the boil, reduce the heat, cover and simmer for 10 minutes until all the water is absorbed. Take off the heat and leave to stand, covered, until you need it.

Preheat the oven to 350°F/180°C. Combine the flakes and thyme leaves and set aside.

Whisk together the oil, honey and lime or lemon juice.

Rinse the quails, remove any feathers and pat dry with kitchen paper. Tie the ends of the drumsticks together with kitchen string and push the tip of the wing behind the breast. Season with salt and pepper, then brush the quails generously with the honey mixture.

Sprinkle the flakes liberally all over the quails gently pressing them on, and then drizzle the rest of the honey mixture on top.

Place on a baking tray and roast for 20–30 minutes until golden and cooked, remove from the oven, cover with foil and keep warm.

Heat the extra oil in a large frying pan. Lightly crush the cardamom pods and throw them into the pan with the ginger, garlic, curry leaves and as many chillies as you like. Stir and cook for about 1–2 minutes until fragrant.

Stir in the quinoa, season with salt and continue cooking until the quinoa is heated through. Toss in the cilantro then serve on a large platter with the quails on top and lime juice squeezed over.

Fragrant Roast Duck with Radish Salad

Place the quinoa in a medium saucepan with the water. Bring to the boil, reduce the heat, cover and simmer for 10 minutes until the water is absorbed. Take off the heat and leave to stand covered for 10–15 minutes then cool completely.

Mix together the five spice powder, ginger, cinnamon, chilli flakes, garlic, soy sauce, honey, cooking wine and sugar.

Prepare the duck by rinsing well inside and out and removing any feathers, excess fat, etc.

Place duck in the sink over a roasting rack, prick the skin all over with a metal skewer then carefully pour boiling water from a completely filled kettle all over the duck (this helps to drain off some of the fat).

Pat dry with kitchen paper and, when cooled, rub the marinade all over and leave to marinate for at least 1 hour, the longer the better.

Preheat the oven to 375°F/190°C and roast duck for 30 minutes. Reduce heat to 350°F/180°C and continue roasting for another 1 hour to an 1 hour 10 minutes, until cooked and browned all over. When cooked, cover with foil and rest for 15 minutes before serving.

While the duck is baking, prepare the salad by placing the cooled quinoa into a bowl with the radishes, cucumbers, celery, chillies, cilantro, rice vinegar, oil and lime juice. Toss well and adjust seasoning if you think it's necessary.

Slice the duck into pieces and serve on top of the salad, garnished with extra cilantro leaves

1 cups quinoa, rinsed and
   drained
2 cups water
1 teaspoon five spice powder
1 teaspoon ground ginger
½ teaspoon cinnamon
1 teaspoon dried chilli flakes
2 cloves garlic, finely chopped
2 tablespoons tamari soy sauce
2 tablespoons honey
2 tablespoons Shaoxing (Chinese)
   cooking wine
½ teaspoon sugar
1 x 4 lb 6oz/2 kg duck

SALAD
6 radishes, sliced
3 cucumbers, cubed
2 stalks celery, sliced
2 long red chillies, chopped
½ cup chopped cilantro/coriander
3 tablespoons rice wine vinegar
1 tablespoon oil
Juice ½–1 lime
Extra cilantro/coriander leaves, to
   garnish

Seafood

Note *I find fish cooked this way is always a great hit and a good way to get kids to eat fish. As much as I love fish and chips, you really can't beat this healthier version.*

Lemon and Chive–crumbed Fish Fillets with Tossed Quinoa Salad

Serves 4-6

Combine the quinoa flakes with the lemon zest, chives, chilli flakes (if using), and salt and pepper.

Place the quinoa flour into a bowl. Dust the fish fillets with the quinoa flour then dip into the beaten egg.

Press the fish into the quinoa flake mixture and coat well.

Heat the oil in a large frying pan until hot, and gently shallow-fry the fillets on a medium–high heat until they are golden and cooked about 3–5 minutes each side, depending on the thickness of the fish.

Remove from the pan and drain on kitchen paper, then serve hot with a good squeeze of lemon juice and the Tossed Quinoa Salad.

Continued on page 162

2½ cups quinoa flakes

Zest of 1 large lemon

3 tablespoons chopped chives

½–1 teaspoon chilli flakes (optional)

Salt and freshly cracked black pepper

1 cup quinoa flour

2 lb 4 oz/1 kg boneless fish fillets

2–3 extra large eggs, lightly beaten

Oil, for shallow-frying

Pepper

Lemon juice, to serve

SALAD

⅔ cup quinoa, rinsed and drained

1⅓ cups water

Selection of your favourite green
  salad leaves

1 cucumber, halved and sliced

1–2 tomatoes, cut into thin
  wedges

1 small red onion, halved then
  thinly sliced

Extra virgin olive oil

Lemon juice

Salt and freshly cracked black
  pepper

Place the quinoa in a small saucepan with the water. Bring to the boil, reduce the heat, cover and simmer for 10 minutes until all the water is absorbed. Take off the heat and leave to stand, covered, for 10 minutes before cooling completely.

To finish off the salad, toss together the cooled, cooked quinoa with the other salad ingredients.

Note *I find that coating the fish cakes with the quinoa flakes gives an added crunch and helps them remain moist and not go rubbery.*

Thai Fish Cakes

Makes about 20

Mix the quinoa flakes and cilantro together and set aside.

Place the onion, garlic, chillies, galangal, lemongrass and kaffir lime leaf into a food processor and process until the ingredients are finely minced.

Remove any bones from the fish, cut into chunks and add to the processor with the egg, cilantro, cumin and fish sauce and continue processing until you get a well combined mixture that still has some texture to it.

Place the mixture into a bowl and mix in the beans.

Roll out spoonfuls of mixture into a ball and flatten slightly then press into the flake and coriander mixture.

Heat some oil until hot and shallow-fry the fish cakes until golden on both sides, about 2 minutes each side. Take care not to overcook them.

Remove with a slotted spoon and place on kitchen paper. Serve immediately with fresh lime juice and/or sweet chilli sauce.

1 cup quinoa flakes

2 tablespoons finely chopped cilantro/coriander leaves

1 small red onion, chopped

4 cloves garlic, chopped

1–2 red chillies

1 knob about 1 in/2.5 cm galangal or ginger, sliced

1 stalk lemongrass, sliced

1 kaffir lime leaf, thinly sliced

17½ oz/500 g white fish fillets

1 extra large egg

3 tablespoons chopped cilantro/coriander roots and leaves

½ teaspoon ground cumin powder

2–3 tablespoons fish sauce

3 oz/90 g fresh green beans, very thinly sliced

Oil for frying

Lime juice, for serving

Sweet chilli sauce, for serving

Rainbow Trout with Almonds and Tarragon

 Serves 2

1½ oz/45 g flaked almonds

1 large tomato

1½ oz/45 g butter

4 scallions/spring onions, finely
    chopped

⅔ cup quinoa flakes

2 cloves garlic, finely chopped

1 tablespoon tarragon, chopped

1 tablespoon baby capers,
    drained

Juice of ½ a lemon

Salt and freshly cracked pepper

2 rainbow trout, scaled and gutted,
    about 12 oz/350 g each

Extra virgin olive oil, for
    drizzling

Lemon juice, for drizzling

Salt and freshly cracked black
    pepper

Tarragon sprigs, for garnish

Lemon wedges, for garnish

Place the almonds in a small non-stick frying pan and gently toast until golden. There is no need to add any oil or butter to the pan but keep an eye on them and toss regularly, as they can burn very quickly. Remove from the heat and transfer onto a plate.

Preheat the oven to 375°F/190°C and line a baking tray with non-stick baking parchment/paper.

Skin the tomato by cutting a small cross at the bottom and then plunging the tomato into boiling water, leave for about 30 seconds then remove. Skin should peel off quite easily. Chop the tomato finely and set aside.

Melt the butter in a medium-sized frying pan, add the scallions and cook on medium-high heat for 1–2 minutes until they start to change colour.

Stir in the quinoa flakes and garlic and cook 2–3 minutes, tossing regularly to coat the flakes in the butter and scallions.

Mix in the tomato, tarragon, capers, some lemon juice and two-thirds of the almonds. Season well with salt and pepper and cool slightly.

Season inside of each fish with a little salt and pepper and fill each one with the stuffing mixture, then secure the opening with metal skewers. Depending on the size of the fish you may have some stuffing mixture left over: wrap in foil and place on the tray with the fish to cook.

Place the fish on the baking tray, drizzle with some extra virgin olive oil, lemon juice and season with salt and pepper. Bake for 20–30 minutes until the trout is cooked.

Serve garnished with a scattering of the remaining almonds, some sprigs of tarragon and lemon wedges.

Steamed Ginger Fish with Sizzling oil

Serves 2

1½ cups quinoa, rinsed and
   drained

3 cups water

4 pieces thick fish fillets, about
   7 oz/200 g each

1 knob of ginger, peeled and cut into
   very thin matchsticks

2 tablespoons tamari soy sauce,
   plus extra for serving

2 tablespoons oil

6 scallions/spring onions, sliced

2 long red or green chillies, de-
   seeded and finely chopped

3 cloves garlic, finely chopped

1 tablespoon fresh ginger, chopped
   (extra)

3 extra large eggs, lightly beaten

2 scallions/spring onions, cut into
   thin strips (extra)

Fresh cilantro/coriander leaves, for
   garnish

Sliced chillies, for garnish

SIZZLING OIL

4 tablespoons oil

1 teaspoon sesame oil

2 cloves garlic, peeled and sliced

Place the quinoa in a medium saucepan with the water. Bring to the boil, reduce the heat, cover and simmer for 10 minutes until all the water is absorbed. Leave to stand, covered, for 10 minutes.

Place the fish on a plate and cover with the slivers of ginger and sprinkle with the soy sauce then place the plate into a steamer over a saucepan or wok of gently simmering water.

Cover and steam the fish for 10–12 minutes or until almost completely cooked, turn off the heat and leave in the steamer, covered, until you finish preparing the quinoa.

To prepare the quinoa, heat the oil in a large frying pan or wok until hot, add the scallions, chillies, garlic and extra ginger and cook, stirring regularly, for 2–3 minutes until fragrant.

Stir in the quinoa and toss for about 2–3 minutes until well coated with the other ingredients and heated right through.

Pour in the eggs and keep tossing and mixing the eggs with the quinoa until the eggs are cooked. Taste and season with salt if need be and keep warm until you finish off the fish.

To finish off the fish, place the fish on to a serving dish with a little of the juices and garnish with the thin strips of scallions and soy sauce.

To make the sizzling oil, place the oils into a pan and heat until really hot, stir in the garlic for just a few seconds then pour over the fish.

Garnish the fish with cilantro leaves and chillies then serve with the quinoa.

Note *You can use peeled shrimp/prawns if you prefer. Turmeric is considered to be a powerful natural anti-inflamatory and antioxidant. In Chinese and Indian medicine, curcumin, the active ingredient in turmeric, is considered to be highly beneficial in treating certain ailments.*

Yellow Shrimp with Peas

Serves 4

Heat the oil in a large frying pan and sauté leek until soft.

Stir in the garlic and turmeric (it's a good idea to wear gloves when grating the turmeric otherwise you will have yellow fingers for a few days) and continue cooking for 1–2 minutes.

Add the quinoa and water or stock, and season with salt and pepper to taste and give it a good stir. Cover with a lid or foil, reduce the heat and simmer for about 8 minutes.

Add the shrimp, bring back to the boil, reduce the heat and continue cooking, covered, for another 10 minutes, until the shrimp turn pink and most of the liquid has been absorbed.

Add the frozen peas, cover and cook for another 5 minutes. Turn off the heat and leave to stand for about 5–10 minutes before serving with lots of lemon juice squeezed over and garnished with fresh parsley and lemon wedges.

2 tablespoons extra virgin olive
  oil
1 leek, washed and finely sliced
4–5 cloves garlic, finely chopped
2 tablespoons fresh turmeric,
  coarsely grated
1½ cups quinoa grain
3¼ cups hot water or fish stock
Salt and freshly cracked black
  pepper
12½ oz/750 g fresh green shrimp/
  prawns, left unpeeled
¾ cup frozen peas
2 tablespoons chopped flat-leaf
  parsley
Lemon juice and wedges, for
  serving

Note *This is a family favourite in our house; it is just so much lighter to digest than the usual fried rice.*

Fried 'Rice'

Serves 6

1½ cups quinoa, rinsed and
  drained

3 cups water

1 tablespoon oil

2 eggs

1 teaspoon soy sauce

1 tablespoon water

2 tablespoons oil extra

½ teaspoon sesame oil

3 rashers bacon, rind removed and
  diced

17½ oz/500 g green shrimp/
  prawns, peeled and de-veined

8 scallions/spring onions, sliced

½ cup frozen peas

7 oz/200 g fresh baby corn spears
  or 1 x 14 oz/400 g can drained

2–3 tablespoons light tamari soy
  sauce

Soy sauce, for serving

Scallions/spring onions, chopped,
  for serving

Place the quinoa in a small saucepan with the water, bring to the boil, then reduce the heat, cover and simmer for 10 minutes until all the water is absorbed. Remove from heat and spread out onto a tray to cool and dry out completely.

Lightly whisk the eggs with the soy sauce and water. Heat the oil in a wok until hot, add the beaten eggs and swirl around to form an omelette.

When the eggs have set, tilt the wok away from you and, using a spatula, carefully roll up the omelette. Remove from the wok and slice into thin strips and set aside.

Heat the extra oil and sesame oil in the wok, add the bacon, shrimp and scallions, including as much of the green part as is usable. Cook on high heat, stirring constantly, until the prawns change colour and the bacon starts to crisp up.

Add the peas and corn spears and continue stirring for 2–3 minutes.

Stir in the soy sauce and the cooled quinoa and continue cooking for 3–4 minutes until quinoa is heated through. Gently stir in the egg strips and serve with an extra drizzle of soy sauce and chopped scallions.

Shrimp with Mango and Coconut Quinoa

Place the quinoa in a medium saucepan with the coconut milk, water and the lime rind. Bring to the boil, reduce the heat, cover and simmer on low heat for about 12–15 minutes until all the liquid is absorbed. Leave to stand, covered, for 10 minutes while you prepare the shrimp.

Heat the oil in a large frying pan and sauté the eschallots, garlic and chilli until soft.

Stir in the shrimp and cook until they turn pink and are cooked.

Add the lime juice, fish sauce and water, and cook for 1–2 minutes.

Stir in the mangoes and cilantro, and cook until the mangoes are heated through and the sauce starts to thicken. Taste, then season with salt and pepper if you need to.

Fluff the quinoa with a fork and serve topped with the shrimp. Serve with a lime wedge and squeeze a little extra lime juice on top.

1½ cups quinoa, rinsed and drained

1½ cups coconut milk

1½ cups water

1 piece of lime rind

2 tablespoons oil

2 large eschallots/French onions, finely chopped

4 cloves garlic, finely chopped

1–2 long red or green chillies, sliced

12½ oz/750 g green shrimp/ prawns, peeled and de-veined

Juice of 1 lime

1 tablespoon fish sauce

½ cup warm water

2 fresh mangoes, peeled and cubed

Small handful cilantro/coriander leaves, roughly chopped

Salt and freshly cracked black pepper

4 lime wedges, for serving

Lime juice, extra, for serving

Note *This is a very quick dish to throw together, especially if you like or, should I dare say, love, anchovies. Leave them out if you don't like them, as this dish is still worth making. If you are using calamari that you have cleaned yourself, cook the heads and tentacles as well as the hoods.*

Whole Calamari with Mediterranean Savoury Quinoa

Serves 4

Place the quinoa in a saucepan with the water. Bring to the boil, reduce the heat, cover and simmer for 10 minutes until all the water is absorbed.

Remove from the heat and rest covered for 10 minutes while you prepare the rest of the dish.

Heat the oil in a large frying pan and sauté the anchovies for 1–2 minutes until they start to break up. They will start to spit and sizzle quite a bit at this stage, so take care.

Stir in the garlic and chilli and cook for about 2 minutes until the garlic starts to change colour then add the capers and give the pan a good stir or toss.

Stir in the quinoa and mix so as to completely coat all the other ingredients and continue cooking long enough to heat through. Remove from the heat, stir through the parsley and keep warm while you cook the calamari.

Place a long-bladed knife into each calamari tube then, using a very sharp knife, cut slices across and through the width of each one until you have a calamari that looks like a concertina (placing the knife inside each tube enables you to cut right through just one side of the calamari without affecting the other side).

Season the quinoa flour with salt and pepper and heat enough oil in a frying pan to shallow-fry. Dust the calamari in the seasoned flour and fry until golden, about 3 minutes on each side.

Serve the savoury quinoa on a large platter and drape the calamari on top. Squeeze some lemon juice on top and a light sprinkle of extra virgin olive oil.

Garnish with lemon wedges.

1½ cups quinoa, rinsed and drained
3 cups water
2–3 tablespoons extra virgin olive oil
6–10 anchovies, chopped
4 cloves garlic, finely sliced
2–3 long red chillies, sliced
3 tablespoons capers, drained
A good handful flat-leaf parsley, roughly chopped
12 whole baby calamari tubes
1 cup quinoa flour
Salt and freshly cracked pepper
Extra virgin olive oil, for frying
Lemon juice, for serving
Extra virgin olive oil, for serving
Lemon wedges, for garnish

Stuffed Squid

4 cleaned large squid tubes

1 cup quinoa, rinsed and drained

2 cups water

2 tablespoons extra virgin olive
   oil

1 small onion, grated

2 cloves garlic, grated

2 fresh tomatoes, grated

¼ cup water

2 tablespoons chopped flat-leaf
   parsley

Salt and freshly cracked black
   pepper

1 x 14 oz/400 g can diced
   tomatoes

2 cloves garlic, finely grated

1 heaped teaspoon dried oregano
   leaves

2 tablespoons extra virgin olive
   oil

Salt and freshly cracked black
   pepper

Parsley, finely chopped, for
   garnish

To clean the squid, gently pull and separate the head from the hood. The insides should come away with the head including the ink sac. Remove the fine cartilage and gently pull away the very fine skin. The wings will come away with the skin. Cut out the eyes and remove the beak, which is in the centre of the tentacles, by pushing it up and away. Cut off a small piece at the base of the hood to allow water to freely run through and clean out anything that may be left behind. Rinse the cleaned calamari thoroughly in cold water.

Place quinoa in a small saucepan with the water. Bring to the boil, reduce the heat, cover and simmer for 10 minutes until all the water is absorbed.

In the meantime, heat the oil in a large frying pan and sauté the onion until golden, stir in the garlic and cook for 30 seconds.

Add the tomatoes with their juices, water and parsley, then season with salt and pepper. Cook for about 3–4 minutes until thick, then stir in the quinoa and allow to cool a little.

Fill each hood of the squid tube with the filling (try not to pack too tightly as the quinoa will continue to expand during baking) and secure the opening with a toothpick.

Preheat the oven to 375°F/190°C.

Mix together the canned tomatoes with the garlic, oregano and the extra virgin olive oil, and season with salt and pepper.

Place the stuffed squid in a baking dish and pour the tomato mixture over them. If you cleaned the squid yourself and you have the tentacles, throw them into the dish as well or alternatively chop them up finely and add to the stuffing mixture when you are sautéing the onion.

Bake for about 20–25 minutes. There will be a little shrinkage of the squid during cooking.

Serve with a sprinkle of chopped flat-leaf parsley.

Note Although not exactly the same as a regular pizza, this is a quick and easy way to make a gluten/wheat-free version. There is no kneading or resting of dough required and I like the nutty taste of this dough

Smoked Salmon Pizza

Serves 2

2 cups quinoa flour

1 teaspoon baking powder

½ teaspoon baking soda/
 bicarbonate of soda

½ teaspoon ground oregano

1 teaspoon garlic salt

⅔ cup warm water (approx.)

2 tablespoons extra virgin olive
 oil

TOPPING

1 small red onion, sliced thinly

Juice of ½ lime

5 oz/150 g cream cheese

Arugula/rocket leaves

5 oz/150 g smoked salmon, thinly
 sliced

9 oz/250 g bocconcini cheese, torn
 into pieces

2 tablespoons capers

Extra virgin olive oil, for
 drizzling

Freshly cracked black pepper

Preheat the oven to 400°F/200°C.

Sift flour into a bowl with the baking powder and baking soda, stir in the oregano and garlic salt, then make a well in the centre.

Pour the water and oil in the well and with the tips of your fingers slowly incorporate the flour with the oil and water until the dough comes together and you have a workable dough that holds together. If the dough is too dry, add a little more water or vice versa.

Place the dough on a floured surface and shape into a flat disc. Place the disc onto a sheet of non-stick baking parchment/paper and roll out the pastry into a thin free form round or square shape, then place with the baking paper on a baking tray. (I find the pastry is much easier to handle and move around if on baking paper. You may find that the pastry may split along the edges as you roll it out: if that happens just pinch the sides together).

Bake the pizza base for 15–20 minutes.

In the meantime, place the onion into a bowl with the lime juice and leave to stand for about 15 minutes.

Take the pizza out of the oven and spread with some cream cheese, then top with the rocket leaves, salmon, bocconcini (or bits of cream cheese) capers and the onion.

Drizzle a little extra virgin olive oil on top and sprinkle with lots of cracked pepper. Serve immediately.

Note This has been a regular dish in my family for years. I used to use wheat flour but swapped over to quinoa flour when I discovered it. It works just as well and you can't tell the difference at all. Everyone I have served this to absolutely loves it.

Tuna Mornay with Crunchy Topping

Serves 4

1 x 14½ oz/425 g canned tuna in
    brine or spring water

1 oz/30 g butter

3 tablespoons quinoa flour

1 teaspoon curry powder

1¼ cups milk

Salt and pepper

½–¾ cup tasty or mild cheese,
    grated

3 cups cornflakes

1 cup tasty or mild cheese, grated,
    extra

1 teaspoon butter

Preheat the oven to 350°F/180°C.

Drain and flake the tuna and place into a medium ovenproof casserole dish.

Melt the butter in a saucepan, then stir in the flour and curry powder to form a roux.

Slowly pour in the milk, stirring constantly until sauce starts to thicken and bubble. Season with salt and pepper then stir in the cheese and cook for about 2 minutes, until the cheese has melted into the sauce and the sauce is thick and bubbly.

Pour the sauce over tuna and mix thoroughly to combine.

In a separate bowl, lightly crush the cornflakes and mix with the extra cheese and sprinkle over the tuna.

Dot with a little butter and place in the oven to bake for about 15–20 minutes or until topping is golden and crispy.

Salmon with a Mediterranean Crunchy Topping

Serves 4

Preheat the oven to 350°F/180°C. Line a roasting tray with baking parchment/paper.

Trim the salmon fillets to an even shape and place, skin side down, on the baking parchment/paper in the roasting tray.

Place the sundried tomatoes, garlic, chilli, basil, chives, olives and cheese into a food processor with the juice and zest of a lemon and the oil.

Process until you have the ingredients finely chopped and combined, but not mushy.

Taste and season with salt and pepper if necessary, then combine this mixture with the quinoa flakes and mix well. Mixture should hold together when pressed between your fingertips.

Divide the mixture into four and spread evenly on top of each fillet.

Drizzle with a little extra virgin olive oil and roast for 15–20 minutes until the topping is golden and the salmon is cooked. Salmon should not be overcooked

Serve with a squeeze of lemon juice and garnish with some fresh basil leaves.

4 salmon fillets, about 7 oz/200 g each, with skin on

2 oz/60 g sundried tomatoes

2–3 cloves garlic

1 long red chilli

Small handful basil leaves

3 tablespoons chopped chives

2 oz/60 g pitted black kalamata olives

1 oz/30 g parmesan cheese

Juice and zest of 1 lemon

2 tablespoons extra virgin olive oil or oil from the tomatoes

Salt and pepper to taste

1⅓ cups quinoa flakes

Extra virgin olive oil, to drizzle

Lemon wedges, to serve

Fresh basil leaves, to garnish

Sweet things

Note *These biscuits are so easy to make and are very popular in our household. I often have to make a double quantity as they just disappear and don't stay long enough in the container. They are great for school lunches or picnics or just to take to somebody's house.*

Pistachio Biscuits

Makes 20–24

1 cup quinoa flour

1½ teaspoons baking powder

1 teaspoon baking soda/bicarbonate
  of soda

1 cup quinoa flakes

4 oz/125 g shelled, unsalted
  pistachio nuts, chopped but not
  too finely

1 cup superfine/caster sugar

5 oz/150 g unsalted butter,
  melted

1 teaspoon vanilla bean paste or
  extract

1 extra large egg, lightly beaten

Preheat the oven to 350°F/180°C and line two baking trays with non-stick baking parchment/paper.

Sift the flour, baking powder and baking soda into a bowl, then stir in the quinoa flakes, chopped pistachio nuts and sugar.

Pour in the melted butter and vanilla, mix well, then stir in the egg and mix everything together until you have a mixture that holds together when pressed between your fingertips.

Take spoonfuls of the mixture, the size of a walnut, and lightly roll into a ball then place onto the prepared trays and lightly flatten.

The biscuits will spread during baking so leave enough space between each one on the tray.

Bake for 10–12 minutes until golden. Cool completely on the trays before removing and storing in an airtight container. Biscuits are crisp on the outside and chewy on the inside.

These biscuits keep well in an airtight container.

Note *The dough for these biscuits can be frozen and taken out when required.*

Chewy Christmas Biscuits

Makes about 30

4 oz/125 g dried apricots, coarsely
chopped

4 oz/125 g golden raisins, coarsely
chopped

3½ oz/100 g candied/glacé cherries,
coarsely chopped

1½ oz/40 g slivered almonds,
chopped

Juice and grated rind of 1 orange

5 oz/150 g unsalted butter, softened
at room temperature

⅔ cup superfine/caster sugar

1 teaspoon vanilla bean paste

1 teaspoon ground cinnamon

⅛ teaspoon ground cloves

1 extra large egg

2 cups quinoa flour

1 teaspoon gluten-free baking
powder

Place the apricots, raisins, cherries and almonds into a bowl with the orange juice and rind. Cover with plastic wrap and allow to stand overnight at room temperature. If possible, give the fruit a quick mix once or twice.

Cream the butter, sugar, vanilla, cinnamon and cloves with an electric mixer until light and creamy, then add the egg and continue beating until it is incorporated into the mixture.

Sift the flour and the baking powder together and mix into the butter mixture without over mixing. Then, using a spatula, fold in the fruit.

Divide the mixture evenly in half then place each half along the edge of some plastic wrap and roll into a log about 10 in/25 cm long and refrigerate for a few hours or overnight.

Preheat the oven to 300°F/150°C.

Cut each log into about ½ in/1 cm slices and place onto two ungreased baking trays. Bake for 15–20 minutes until lightly golden. Remove onto a cooling rack to cool completely.

These biscuits are soft and chewy and will keep in an airtight container for about a week.

Chocolate Fudge Puddings

Serves 4

Preheat the oven to 350°F/180°C and lightly grease 4 x 1-cup capacity ovenproof ramekins with butter.

Sift flour, baking powder, cocoa and sugar into a bowl.

Add in the egg, milk, vanilla and butter and, using electric beaters, beat everything together until smooth.

Divide the mixture evenly between the prepared ramekins.

Make the topping by combining the brown sugar and sifted cocoa powder into a jug then slowly whisk in the boiling water until smooth.

Slowly and gently pour the topping over the top of each pudding and place the ramekins on a baking tray for easier handling. I find that pouring the topping onto the puddings over the back of a spoon prevents any large holes or unevenness forming.

Bake for about 20–25 minutes or until the puddings are firm but bounces back when pressed in the centre. Leave to sit for 10 minutes before serving as this allows the sauce to thicken.

Serve with a dollop of fresh cream. Puddings are best eaten when they are made, but leftover puddings (if there are any) can be re-heated.

1 cup quinoa flour

2 teaspoons gluten-free baking powder

⅓ cup cocoa powder

¾ cup superfine/caster sugar

1 extra large egg

⅔ cup milk

1 teaspoon vanilla bean paste or extract

2½ oz/75 g butter, melted

Fresh cream, for serving (optional)

TOPPING

¾ cup cup brown sugar, firmly packed

¼ cup cocoa powder, sifted

1¼ cups boiling water

Note *These are a lovely special treat that everyone in the family can enjoy. You can add a few drops of peppermint essence for a twist on the after-dinner mint or, if making these for adults only, add 1–2 tablespoons of your favourite liquor.*

Chocolate Bites

Makes about 30 pieces

Lightly toast the quinoa flakes in a medium- to large-sized non-stick frying pan over a low-medium heat. You need a pan that has enough surface space for the flakes to toast as evenly as possible. Keep an eye on the flakes by regularly moving them around the pan as they can burn very easily. Once they turn a light golden colour—you will be able to smell them at this point—remove from the heat and transfer the toasted flakes into a dish to cool completely.

Line an 8 in/20 cm baking tray with aluminium foil and set aside.

Place the chocolate, butter, vanilla and golden syrup into a medium-sized saucepan and stir over low heat until the chocolate and butter have melted.

Stir in the toasted quinoa, cooled quinoa flakes and almonds then pour the chocolate mixture into the prepared tin.

Refrigerate overnight or until set into a firm consistency, then cut into bite-sized pieces to serve.

Store these chocolate bites in the refrigerator at all times in a covered container.

¾ cup quinoa flakes

7 oz/200 g dark chocolate, chopped

3½ oz/100 g milk chocolate, chopped

4 oz/125 g butter

1 teaspoon vanilla extract

2 tablespoons golden syrup

1 cup Toasted Quinoa (see recipe)

2 oz/60 g flaked almonds

Orange, Coconut and Cherry Jam Cake

Serves 6–8

4 oz/125 g unsalted butter, softened
  at room temperature

¾ cup superfine/caster sugar

Grated rind of 1 orange

1 teaspoon vanilla bean paste

2 extra large eggs, separated

2 cups quinoa flour

1 teaspoon gluten-free baking
  powder

Juice of 1 orange

¼ cup milk

¾ cup shredded coconut

9 oz/250 g of your favourite cherry
  jam or spread

Preheat the oven to 350°F/180°C and grease a 9 x 5 in/23 x 25½ cm loaf tin.

Cream the butter and sugar together until light and creamy. Mix in the orange rind and vanilla then add in the egg yolks and beat well.

Sift the flour and baking powder together and stir into the creamed mixture alternately with the juice and milk (don't worry if mixture looks a little curdled)

Gently fold in the coconut and cherry jam. Beat egg whites until soft peaks form and lightly fold into the cake mixture.

Pour the mixture into the well-greased, prepared loaf tin and bake for 50–60 minutes or so, depending on your oven. The cake is cooked when tested by inserting a metal skewer and it comes out clean.

Apple Pudding

Preheat the oven to 350°F/180°C and lightly grease a deep 64 fl oz/2-litre ovenproof dish with butter.

Mix the apples with the brown sugar, lemon rind, juice and water in a saucepan and bring to the boil. Cover and simmer for about 7–10 minutes or until the apples are tender.

In the meantime, cream the butter, caster sugar and vanilla until light and creamy. Add the eggs and mix well.

Sift in the flour, baking powder and baking soda, and, using a spatula, fold into the egg mixture, together with the almond meal and milk.

As soon as the apples are tender, place them into the prepared dish while they are still hot and drop spoonfuls of the flour mixture on top.

Sprinkle the flaked almonds on top and bake for about 20–25 minutes until the sponge and almonds are golden.

Serve warm or cold with custard.

5 large cooking apples, peeled, cored and sliced

½ cup brown sugar

Grated rind of 1 lemon

1 tablespoon lemon juice

¼ cup water

2½ oz/75 g butter at room temperature

½ cup superfine/caster sugar

1 teaspoon vanilla bean paste or extract

2 extra large eggs

1 cup quinoa flour

½ teaspoon baking powder

½ teaspoon baking soda/ bicarbonate of soda

1 oz/30 g almond meal

3 tablespoons milk

3 oz/90 g flaked almonds

Custard, for serving

Note *I love the look of whole peanuts through these bars, however, if the are too big, they can be a bit difficult to cut so a rough chop is not a bad idea. You can also replace the peanuts with other nuts or leave them out altogether. These bars are great when you need a quick snack.*

Chocolate, Seeds and Nut Snack Bars

Makes about 20

Preheat the oven to 350°F/180°C and lightly grease a 12 x 7½ in/29 x 19 cm slice tin then line with baking parchment/paper. Greasing the tin first helps the parchment stay in place.

Sift the flour and baking powder into a large bowl then stir in the quinoa flakes and sugar; mix well, making sure you break up any lumps in the sugar.

Add the chocolate chips, peanuts, almonds, pepitas and sunflower seeds and mix well to combine everything together.

Pour the melted butter, vanilla and the eggs over the flour mixture and stir really well until everything is combined and not dry. Evenly distribute the butter and egg throughout the flour mixture.

Using the back of a spoon, press the mix firmly into the prepared tin. Scatter as many of the extra chocolate chips over the top as you like, and bake for about 20–25 minutes until golden.

Remove from the oven and leave to cool in the tin for about 15 minutes and then cut into desired sized bars. Leave to cool in the tin for a little longer, then carefully remove the slice with the paper and place on a cooling rack to cool completely.

¾ cup quinoa flour

1 teaspoon gluten-free baking powder

1 cup quinoa flakes

1 cup brown sugar

4 oz/125 g chocolate chips, dark or milk

4 oz/125 g raw or roasted peanuts, roughly chopped (see note)

2 oz/60 g blanched, slivered almonds

4 oz/125 g pepitas/pumpkin seeds

4 oz/125 g sunflower seeds

2 oz/60 g butter, melted

1 teaspoon vanilla bean paste

2 extra large eggs, lightly beaten

Chocolate chips, extra

Note *I tend to serve this pudding cold as that is how my family prefer it. It will thicken and become creamier after it has been refrigerated. How much cardamom you use depends on taste. I have found that the ground store-bought cardamom is not as strong in flavour as when I use the pods. Using a mortar and pestle, smash the pods, discard the pods and grind the seeds to a fine powder.*

Creamy Sultana Pudding

Serves 4-6

1 cup quinoa, rinsed and drained

4½ cups milk

¼ cup superfine/caster sugar

½ cup brown sugar

½–¾ teaspoons ground cardamom

¼ teaspoon ground nutmeg

4 oz/125 g sultanas or golden raisins

1 teaspoon vanilla extract

Place the quinoa in a large saucepan over low-medium heat with the milk, sugars, spices, sultanas and vanilla. Stir until the sugars dissolve.

Slowly bring to the boil, but be careful that the heat is not too high, or the milk could curdle. Reduce heat to low, cover and simmer for 30–35 minutes stirring occasionally until quinoa is cooked and the mixture is thick and creamy.

Remove from the heat and leave to stand, covered, for about 20–30 minutes to cool and continue to soften and absorb more liquid.

Pour into individual bowls or one large serving bowl and serve warm or refrigerate for a few hours, or overnight, and serve cold.

Note *This is one of the easiest cakes you can make and not only is it gluten/wheat-free, but it is also completely egg and dairy free. Great spread with a little butter or just as it is. I just like a cup of hot tea with mine.*

Date, Ginger and Walnut Loaf

Preheat the oven to 325°F/160°C and grease a 8 x 4 x 2 in/20 x 10 x 5 cm loaf tin (preferably non-stick) with butter.

Place the dates, ginger, sugar, walnuts, vanilla, butter and baking soda into a bowl.

Pour the boiling water over the date mixture, stir well and leave to sit for about 10 minutes.

Sift the flour and baking powder together and fold into the date mixture. Pour into prepared loaf tin and bake for about 1 hour to 1 hour and 10 minutes. Cover the cake with foil if, after 50 minutes, you feel it is browning too quickly.

Test the cake with a metal skewer after about 55 minutes; when the skewer comes out clean the cake is ready. Leave in the tin for 10–15 minutes before turning out to cool on a wire rack. It is best to use a serrated knife when slicing the cake.

12 oz/350 g dried dates, roughly chopped into large pieces

¾ cup raw sugar

3 oz/90 g preserved ginger, chopped

2 oz/60 g walnuts, chopped

1 teaspoon vanilla bean paste or extract

2 tablespoons soft butter

1 teaspoon baking soda/bicarbonate of soda

1 cup boiling water

1½ cups quinoa flour

½ teaspoon gluten-free baking powder

Chocolate and Orange Soufflé

Serves 4

Preheat the oven to 350°F/180°C and grease 4 x 1-cup capacity ramekins with butter.

Cream the sugar, egg yolks and the 1 whole egg until pale and creamy.

Stir in the flour then pour in the milk and whisk until smooth.

Transfer to a saucepan and bring to the boil over a low heat, stirring constantly until the mixture thickens.

Break the chocolate into small pieces; add to the custard with the orange juice, zest and coffee. Take the mixture off the heat and stir until the chocolate melts.

In a clean bowl, whisk the egg whites until stiff, and gently fold into the chocolate mixture.

Pour the mixture into the prepared ramekins, then run your finger tip along the inside and top of the rim of each ramekin to separate the mixture from the dish so that the soufflé will rise more during baking.

Bake for about 30–35 minutes until the soufflés have risen and are firm to the touch.

Dust with powdered sugar and serve immediately with some fresh raspberries or strawberries on the side of the dish.

½ cup superfine/caster sugar

3 extra large eggs, separated

1 extra large egg, whole

4 tablespoons quinoa flour

11½ oz/350 ml milk

7 oz/200 g dark chocolate, broken into small pieces

Zest and juice 1 large orange

½ teaspoon instant coffee

Confectioners'/icing sugar, for dusting

Fresh raspberries or strawberries for serving

Note Traditionally a cheesecake is made with a biscuit base. The base in this recipe is made using quinoa flour and flakes, which makes it gluten/wheat-free and delicious. Don't be concerned if the cheesecake splits after baking—they sometimes do that.

Sour Cream Lemon Cheesecake

Serves 6–8

1 cup quinoa flour

1 cup quinoa flakes

¼ cup raw sugar

1 teaspoon baking powder

1 teaspooon ground cinnamon

5 oz/150 g unsalted butter,
  melted

17½ oz/500 g cream cheese, at
  room temperature

1 cup sour cream

3 extra large eggs

1 cup superfine/caster sugar

Zest of 1 lemon

4 tablespoons lemon juice

1 teaspoon vanilla bean paste or
  extract

Fresh whipped cream, for serving

Fresh strawberries, for garnish

Preheat the oven to 350°F/180°C.

Mix together the flour, flakes, sugar, baking powder and cinnamon until combined. Stir in the melted butter and mix until well combined and moist, and holds together.

Grease and line the base of a 8 in/20 cm round non-stick springform tin. Press the mixture firmly into the base of an and bake for 15 minutes. Remove from the oven and reduce the oven temperature to 325°F/160°C.

Place a small ovenproof bowl of hot water on the bottom rack of the oven. This will provide moisture during the baking time so the cheesecake won't dry out.

Place the cream cheese, sour cream, eggs, sugar, lemon zest, lemon juice and vanilla into a food processor and process until smooth. Don't over-mix.

Pour the cheese mixture onto the crumb base and bake for about 50–55 minutes until the cheesecake is cooked. Cheesecake is ready when the edges are slightly puffed and the centre is slightly wobbly. Cool for at least 30 minutes, then refrigerate for several hours before serving.

Remove from the tin and decorate with whipped cream and fresh strawberries to serve.

Note *These little tarts are best eaten on the day they are made. They are lovely served as a dinner party dessert with some good vanilla ice cream or custard. You can use whatever berries you like, either frozen or fresh. I have used frozen purely for convenience sake, so you can make these little tarts at anytime of the year.*

Orange and Mixed Berry Tarts

Remove the berries from the freezer. Place them in a colander and set aside to partially thaw as you prepare the other ingredients.

Preheat the oven to 325°F/170°C and grease eight round 4 x ¾ in/10 x 2 cm tart tins with butter.

Sift the quinoa flour and baking powder together and combine with the almond meal and sugar in a large bowl. In another bowl, whisk together the egg, milk, vanilla and butter, then stir in the orange zest and juice.

Pour the wet ingredients into the dry ingredients and, using a spatula, gently mix until well combined.

Pour the mixture evenly between tins, filling about three-quarters full. Gently tap the tins on your kitchen bench to remove any air bubbles.

Scatter the berries on top and use your fingertips to rub together the extra zest with the extra sugar and sprinkle on top of each tart.

Bake for about 25–30 minutes.

Leave to stand in the tins for 5–10 minutes before carefully removing the tarts from the tins and cooling on a wire rack.

9 oz/250 g frozen mixed berries

1½ cups quinoa flour

1 teaspoon baking powder

¾ cup ground almond meal

½ cup superfine/caster sugar

1 extra large egg

⅔ cup milk

1 teaspoon vanilla

2 oz/60 g butter, melted

Zest of 1 orange

Juice of half an orange

Zest of 1 orange, for topping

3 tablespoons superfine/caster
   sugar, for topping

Fruit and Nut Slice

9 oz/250 g dried figs, finely
   chopped

Juice and grated rind of 1 large
   orange

3 tablespoons water

1 cup quinoa flour

1 cup quinoa flakes

¼ cup granulated/raw sugar

1 teaspoon baking powder

1 teaspoon ground cinnamon

1 extra large egg

5 oz/150 g unsalted butter,
   melted

3 oz/60 g walnuts, finely chopped

1 extra large egg (extra)

1 extra large egg white

1 teaspoon vanilla bean paste

4 oz/125 g coconut flakes

Preheat the oven to 350°F/180°C and line a 7 x 11½ in/18 x 29 cm slice tin with non-stick baking parchment/paper, letting some hang over the sides.

Place the figs, orange juice, orange rind and water into a small saucepan and cook, covered, over low heat for about 10 minutes until figs soften and are almost sticky.

Mix together the flour, flakes, sugar, baking powder and cinnamon until combined. Stir in the egg and melted butter until the mixture is combined. It should be moist and hold together.

Press the mixture firmly into the base of a prepared tin and bake for 15 minutes. Remove from the oven and spread the fig mixture on top, then sprinkle the walnuts over the figs.

Whisk together the extra egg, egg white and vanilla, then stir in the coconut. Using a fork, spread this mixture over the figs and walnuts. Place the tin in the oven and bake for 25–30 minutes until golden.

Cool in the tin until barely warm, then remove and cut into squares. Alternatively, you could cut into larger squares then halve the squares into triangles.

Note *I love the smell of the spices wafting through the house as this cake is baking. You can serve it warm or cold, and it is lovely with a hot cup of tea or coffee.*

Spiced Tea Cake

Serves 6-8

Preheat the oven to 325°F/160°C and grease a 8 in/20 cm non-stick cake tin.

Sift together the flour, baking powder, baking soda, cinnamon, allspice and nutmeg.

Using electric beaters, cream the butter, vanilla and sugar together until creamy. Add the eggs one at a time, and beat until light and fluffy.

Using a spatula, fold in the flour alternately with the milk then pour the mixture into the prepared tin

Bake for approximately 30–35 minutes or until skewer comes out clean when tested.

Remove the cake from the oven and leave to stand for about 15 minutes before removing from tin and slicing.

Dust the cake with confectioners' sugar and serve warm with a dollop of cream with a little cinnamon sprinkled on top.

1½ cups quinoa flour

1½ teaspoon gluten-free baking powder

1½ teaspoon baking soda/ bicarbonate of soda

2 teaspoons ground cinnamon

1 teaspoon ground allspice

½ teaspoon ground nutmeg

4 oz/125 g butter, softened at room temperature

1 teaspoon vanilla bean paste or extract

1 cup superfine/caster sugar

2 extra large eggs

⅓ cup milk

Confectioners'/icing sugar, for dusting

Cream, for serving

Cinnamon, for sprinkling

acknowledgments

I would like to thank my publisher, Linda Williams, and Fiona Schultz, Managing Director, of New Holland Publishers for their continued support, encouragement and belief in my work. This is our third quinoa cook book together and without you both believing in me it would never have been possible. Linda, thank you for always being there for me.

To my beautiful editor Jodi De Vantier, a very special thank you for being such a joy to work with.

It has always been such a pleasure to work with all the team in New Holland, a huge thank you to all of you, especially Sacha Gratton, Diane Ward and Tracy Loughlin for all your help and hard work throughout the whole process of publishing my books.

Thank you so much to my food stylist, Tracy Rutherford, and Sue Stubbs, my photographer, for all your beautiful and stunning work—it was such a pleasure to work with you.

To my wonderful, ever-encouraging and very understanding family, my husband Graeme, son Chris, daughters Alex and Nikki, their husbands Lachlan and Marcus and my gorgeous grandchildren Madison and Kobe and to my parents, Lina and John, I love and appreciate you all more than you can ever know.

To our beautiful and much loved Zac, we miss you so much; you are always in our thoughts and will always be in our hearts.

Index

First published 2013 by
New Holland Publishers Pty Ltd
London • Cape Town • Sydney • Auckland

Garfield House 86–88 Edgware Road London W2 2EA United Kingdom
Wembley Square First Floor Solan Road Gardens Cape Town 8001 South Africa
1/66 Gibbes Street Chatswood NSW 2067 Australia
218 Lake Road Northcote Auckland New Zealand

www.newhollandpublishers.com

A record of this book is held at the British Library and National Library of Australia

ISBN 9781742574004

Managing director: Fiona Schultz
Publisher: Linda Williams
Project editor: Jodi De Vantier
Designer: Tracy Loughlin
Photographs: Sue Stubbs
Stylist: Tracy Rutherford
Proofreader: Meryl Potter
Production director: Olga Dementiev
Printer: Toppan Leefung Printing Ltd (China)

10 9 8 7 6 5 4 3 2 1

Keep up with New Holland Publishers
on Facebook www.facebook.com/NewHollandPublishers